PLAYS BY WOMEN
VOLUME ONE

Vinegar Tom *by Caryl Churchill,* Dusa, Fish, Stas and Vi *by Pam Gems,* Tissue *by Louise Page,* Aurora Leigh *by Michelene Wandor*

Michelene Wandor is the author of *Understudies,* published in 1981, which took a provocative look at sexual politics in the theatre. Now she has compiled a volume of recent plays by women which offer an indication of the wide range of style and subject matter tackled by women playwrights. Included are Caryl Churchill's *Vinegar Tom,* about witchcraft in the seventeenth century; *Dusa, Fish, Stas and Vi,* an account of the lives of four young women by Pam Gems (author of *Piaf*); Louise Page's *Tissue,* about breast cancer; and *Aurora Leigh,* adapted by Michelene Wandor herself from Elizabeth Barrett Browning's verse novel. Each play has an afterword by its author and the volume opens with an introduction by the editor.

A METHUEN THEATREFILE
in series with
Other Spaces: New Theatre and the RSC, by Colin Chambers
The Plays of Edward Bond, by Tony Coult
Understudies: Theatre and Sexual Politics, by Michelene Wandor

PLAYS BY WOMEN

Volume One

VINEGAR TOM
by
Caryl Churchill

DUSA, FISH, STAS AND VI
by
Pam Gems

TISSUE
by
Louise Page

AURORA LEIGH
by
Michelene Wandor

Edited and introduced by
Michelene Wandor

A Methuen Theatrefile
Methuen · London

This volume first published as a paperback original in 1982 by
Methuen London Ltd, 11 New Fetter Lane, London EC4P 4EE.

Vinegar Tom first published in 1978 by TQ Publications.
Copyright © 1978, 1982 by Caryl Churchill
Song *If You Float* copyright © 1976, 1978, 1982 by Helen Glavin

Dusa, Fish, Stas and Vi first published in an acting edition in 1977 by Samuel French Ltd.
Copyright © 1977, 1982 by Mudeford Plays Ltd.

Tissue first published in this volume. Copyright © 1982 by Louise Page

Aurora Leigh first published in this volume. Copyright © 1982 by Michelene Wandor

Typeset by Expression Typesetters, London N7
Printed in Great Britain by Richard Clay (The Chaucer Press) Ltd, Bungay, Suffolk

ISBN 0 413 50020 9

CONTENTS

Radio and television plays listed in the British Alternative Theatre Directory, edited by Catherine Itzin (John Offord Publications, Ltd).

INTRODUCTION

Why an anthology of plays by women? If one looks at the contents page of any play anthology, one is already halfway to the answer. Such books are largely anthologies of plays by men writers, though most people would not immediately pick that out as a distinguishing factor. We are so used to assuming that a writer is a writer is a writer, that drawing attention to the gender of playwrights might appear at first to be a diversion. And yet it leads to other, very important questions. Why is it that we know of so few women playwrights, when the novel, past and present, boasts so many women in its ranks? A quick roll-call of famous dramatists of the past might just about include Aphra Behn, but more because she is popularly known as the first woman to earn her living by her pen, than because her plays are actually read and performed today.

In fact it doesn't take much digging below the surface to realise that far more women have written plays than is generally assumed. In her book about the first women in the theatre, *Enter the Actress* (1931) Rosamund Gilder writes at some length about Hrotsvitha, a tenth-century Benedictine nun in Saxony, who wrote plays in Latin. Women were an integral part of the *commedia dell'arte* groups in Italy in the sixteenth century, and contributed to the material they performed. Although women were not allowed on the public stage at the time, aristocratic ladies in the reign of Elizabeth I wrote tragedies and translated the classics for the courtly stage. After 1660, when the stage was openly available as a 'career' for actresses, women playwrights followed swiftly; of these Aphra Behn was the most successful, but other women wrote for the two London theatres. Between 1660 and 1720 some sixty plays by women were staged.

Recent research has shown that between 1900 and 1920 around 400 women wrote plays, coinciding with the campaigns for female suffrage, but also very importantly with the agitation in the latter part of the nineteenth century to gain access for women to higher education and the professions. Of course women were not idle as writers between the seventeenth and twentieth centuries. As is clear from any history of literature, women were formative in the development of the novel. The new leisured 'middling' class in the eighteenth century began producing its own culture and developing its own cultural industries: in particular, journalism and book publishing. The latter enabled women of the new leisured class to write novels (and the more private forms of diary and letter-writing); such novels were then read by similar women – a kind of community of women reading and writing in private, the two groups mediated via the public world of publishing and distribution, which remained in the hands of men.

Victorian sexual ideology produced a painfully contradictory status for the woman writer. On the one hand her fiction was praised and valued; on the other, the woman herself was castigated for stepping out of line from the Victorian ideal of silent, decorative womanhood. Economic independence threatened this social image, and women's relative invisibility as female writers was maintained by the male pseudonym, which many women adopted. Of course many women wrote under their own names too, but the very fact that such a 'naming' disguise was necessary indicates how closely related the general social image of gender is to the image of the writer. The very concept of the 'writer' implies *maleness*, so that the sub-category 'woman writer' had to be developed in the nineteenth century to cover a species of creativity that challenged the dominant image. To a great extent we still live under the cloud of gender-confusion in our image of the 'writer', especially in the theatre.

At the end of the nineteenth century women re-entered the theatre as writers also because the theatre itself was undergoing a revolution. The radical naturalism of Ibsen and others, which addressed itself to contemporary social and domestic questions, found support from some English actresses. Often the plays themselves explored the appearance of a 'new' woman. The first substantial wave of feminism was very much in the air. Later the Actresses' Franchise League, founded in 1908, generated plays, monologues and sketches by women and men in support of the suffrage campaign – a kind of suffragette agitprop which drew on the new low-key naturalism of the more sophisticated radical theatre. Women within the theatrical profession became aware of the overt and covert discrimination they faced, and women's theatre groups were formed, one of which lasted well into the 1920s. In the 1930s women wrote plays as part of the nation-wide socialist theatre movement, Unity.

It is clear even from this very sketchy rush through theatrical history that women have written plays. It's just that those plays hardly ever figure as part of our received knowledge about the theatre. It is also clear that at particular periods in history women do emerge as playwrights in the public eye – looking at the Restoration, the early years of this century, the 1930s – it seems that women surface as playwrights when the conditions are right: when there are changes in the dominant sexual morality which benefit the social position of women, when a movement for political change includes a feminist component, or when revolutions in the theatre itself make it possible for women to seize the time and make their own mark. Looking at the last ten years, it seems that all these factors have been in operation, following on from a series of important social changes in post World War Two Britain.

The principle of equal access to higher education for children of all classes was initiated with state support in the 1940s; scientific developments in contraception in the 1950s and 1960s made it easier for women to choose whether and when to have children. In the 1960s a series of events gave rise to the political and cultural upheavals of 1968, which helped crystallise and form the second major wave of feminist struggle this century. In Britain the Women's Liberation Movement formally started in 1969-70. Meanwhile the theatre industry was itself going through another period of change – studio theatres and later the fringe theatre movement and state subsidy – all expanded the range of performance styles and audiences in a manner which paved the way for a new generation of women playwrights.

In the early 1970s many fringe theatre groups (particularly those with a conscious socialist bias) questioned the received class bias of commercial theatre, both in its content and in the audience it reached. Such 'political' groups made their own theatre and found their own audiences. Other groups concentrated on more experimental, avantgarde theatre (mixed-media, later performance art, for example). But although the range of political and aesthetic concerns within the fringe is very varied, the general tendency across the board has been characterised by different attempts to democratise the theatrical process itself, by challenging conventional assumptions about skill and the social division of labour, by reaching out to new audiences, and by giving space to new content, whether it is defined by its class bias, or by developing new theatrical forms (music-theatre, for example).

In many of the theatre collectives of the early 1970s the challenge to the division of labour was sometimes hard to follow through. In the interests of doing away with anything that led to authoritarianism, each group member did a bit of everything (acting, administration, etc). Job preference, ability, skill were subsumed under a notion of democracy which had its heart in the right political place, but which in its turn repressed aspects of individual creativity which are not simply replaceable. The functions of writer and director were seen as subservient to the needs of the group, and although this did (and still can) produce good working relationships between writers and companies, the experiments were more important for the way they drew attention to the relative powerlessness of the performer in most theatrical set-ups. In fact these collectives tended not to consist of skills evenly spread across the work, but to be in fact performer-collectives, or performer-managements. The feminist street- and indoor- theatre of the early 1970s often took on unthinkingly this 'collectivist' ideology, and to some extent this explains why women writers were slow to come to the fore in the early part of the 1970s.

Gradually other women theatre workers became aware of the feminist movement, and it was logical for them to want to include some kind of response to feminism as part of their political/aesthetic projects. This desire uncovered another layer of the division of labour in theatre. While collectives were dealing with traditional hierarchical management authoritarianism, the sexual division of labour was largely ignored. The socialist groups were dominated by men. Women tended to be in the numerical minority, and rarely vocal in defining the nature of the group's work. The all-women's theatre groups which formed from 1974 onwards very consciously decided not to include men because they did not want to have to cope with the tensions of fighting out sexist issues with men in the group, preferring to keep their energies for their work and arguing out the differences among themselves.

As the stringent collectivism of the early 1970s gave way to a more flexible collaborative way of working, the groups began to re-recognise the importance of the writer's and director's skills. Groups (all women, or mainly women, and later mixed groups too) began searching out women writers, looking for plays about women. Looking through the theatre pages of *Time Out*, it is notable that from late 1977- early 1978 onwards more and more plays by women writers were being performed. And it is also interesting to remember that even in the spring of 1973, when a group of us were meeting to plan the first Women's Theatre Festival (at the Almost Free Theatre in London in autumn 1973), we weren't short of plays from which to choose for the three-month season. The submerged women playwrights were there – as they appear always to have been.

****

Traditionally the theatre gives more credit and status to the 'creative' artistic jobs than it does to the merely functional or technical. Thus theatre history celebrates the writer (more easily done anyway, since the texts of plays are published, where a production has no literal record) and the director as the primary initiators. In one sense that is a truism – the writer initiates the text, the director initiates its interpretation. But the very emphasis on these skills as creative as *against* the other skills, often means that the creativity of lighting or set construction are rarely recognised.

It is interesting that as far as the sexual division of labour in the theatre goes, men dominate at both ends of the status scale – in the technological and manual areas of backstage production, and in the artistically authoritative voices of writer and director. In the case of the first, this is consistent with women's relative absence from those skills in industry as a whole; in the case of the second it is consistent with the image of the artist being implicitly male. However, around the middle of the status scale the division is more blurred – for example, women form a fairly high proportion of working designers – between a quarter and a third, although the top designers are almost all male. Women tend to appear in positions of middle-management, associated with jobs like personnel and casting or wardrobe (the 'personal relations' jobs). Finally, women dominate in two areas – in the traditionally female servicing jobs of secretarial and administration, in theatre publicity and of course, where they are irreplaceable because of the gender demands of the job – as actresses. This general discussion of where women generally work in the theatre industry is important because the image of 'woman' in the theatre in general has a direct bearing on the image of the 'woman' writer in particular.

The image of woman as theatre worker is most explicit in the way the actress and the woman in charge of publicity are seen, and in the way they present themselves. The actress's function is divided between her real and highly skilled job as a performer – responding to the specific demands of each play or show – and her ideological function, which is as a symbol of the glamour and excitement of the theatre. It is a paradoxical image, because although the image of the actress appears to combine the acceptable face of feminine appearance and behaviour (with the occasional Wicked Woman to lend salacious overtones) with economic success, in fact the average earnings of actresses are well below the average earnings of actors, in a profession dogged by high unemployment.

The theatre actress is seen as part of the gamut of sexual imagery in our culture, which is represented at its most extreme in advertising. Here all sexuality, but particularly female heterosexuality, are used to lend glamour and desirability to help persuade us to want and buy. It is a very subtle process, but women are at the centre of it – as a crucial part of the imagery. Women are also, however, crucial behind the scenes to service the industry. In the theatre the publicity job is almost always done by a woman because she is at the sales counter, as it were – selling the play to the press, the critics and the rest of the industry. In her low-key glamour way she is there to help sugar the difficult commercial sell, while the image of the actress (which publicity helps create) has higher glamour content. This complex use of female sexuality as part of the industrial process in theatre in no way diminishes from the skills which these jobs involve. But women do not work where they do by simple accident, and the images of femininity and masculinity which are part of the fabric of the society we live in operate in the theatre as well as in the more moneyed glamour world of the television and film industries.

****

It is against this kind of double-edged imagery of woman that the female writer takes her place – the invisible servicing female on the one hand, and the visible, sexually acceptable female on the other. Two images of femininity which place covert limits on the job demarcation and the aspirations of women. We're not helped by the fact that our theatrical tradition of 'great' writers does not have a single woman in it. There isn't yet enough research to provide full answers to questions about the historical and aesthetic place women's plays might have in a history that would include women playwrights. But to make such an assessment one would have to develop an analysis based on the relationship between gender and theatre, as well as taking other matters of class and culture into account. The reality is that plays are written by particular people at particular times, under particular social conditions. If the interests or values of a play carry over from one time to another (as, for example, Shakespeare has done – though he has had his ups and downs of popularity over the centuries) it is because the play catches at social contradictions ('conflicts', in the language of theatre criticism) which can carry reverberations for a contemporary audience. It is not simply because there is something mystical and abstractly 'universal' about particular plays.

A woman writer finding her place in the theatre also implicitly challenges the assumption that because there have been many great and exciting actresses, women have been adequately catered for in plays. The great heroines of Greek tragedy, or in Shakespeare's plays, or more recently in Shaw, have been adduced as proof that there is nothing that women writers can add to the range of theatrical subject matter. Men can write about women, the assumption goes, and if women are not known as playwrights then it is simply because they are not as good as the men. But such an assumption raises questions about who defines what is valid subject matter for plays, what a 'serious' or 'important' subject is, and how women figure within such assumptions. The male playwrights of our classical theatre wrote in a world in which public events were dominated by men, and in which women had at best an ambiguous status, dependent on their class. It is one thing to see Antigone as a female heroine, another to see her as a character, as a particularly poignant and vulnerable cypher via which the issues of honour and loyalty *as they are experienced by men,* are explored. It is not that women cannot sympathise with these concerns, it is not that actresses cannot act them, or that women in the audiences cannot appreciate them. To say that the content of our received theatrical tradition is largely (and often very complexly) male defined, simply re-orients our perspective, and enables us to see a bias that can enrich our understanding of our received tradition, while at the same time recognising that a future theatre which has more women writing for it, will itself introduce new concepts of subject matter.

But until such a time comes, the woman writer will continue to have something of an uphill struggle, and will continue to be seen as something of an anomaly. For example, between the years 1956-1975, only 17 out of 250 produced plays at the Royal Court Theatre (known for its championship of new writing) were written and/ or directed by women. Today women represent around 15% of all playwrights, according to the 1981 edition of the British Alternative Theatre Directory, which will list any playwright who sends in information about him/herself. Such a percentage is not represented in commercial play publishing, which bases its editorial choices largely on commercial success in performance. Women rarely write commercially successful plays and so rarely get their plays published.

By contrast, Samuel French, who publish for the amateur acting market, show a different picture. Amateur dramatic companies have a high proportion of women members (the opposite to professional companies in which women are generally in a minority – to cater for the repertoire of published plays in which women characters are in a minority, etc etc). French's catalogue of plays for all-female casts includes a much higher proportion of women writers, and again it is clear that women do write plays, even though the amateur market still has more male writers. We still are insufficiently visible.

****

The theatre is a social and public art in many senses of the word. It is consumed by its audiences in groups in public, within a short space of time. It may be remembered or read in private, but performance is social and ephemeral. A novelist can write in private and her/his text, once published is available for the individual reader to read in private. The theatre demands something more from its writers. A playwright could take no interest in how a play is produced, but generally people write plays because they get a buzz out of seeing their words realised in three dimensions, and because they enjoy the combination of private creativity and public collaboration which the theatre potentially offers.

A playwright thus must come out more publicly than a novelist; must be more vulnerable to the scrutiny of co-workers. A writer is particularly dependent on having a good working relationship with a director, since it is that collaboration above all which ensures a smooth transition from the privacy of writing to the publicness of performance. The director generally has far more institutional clout than the writer; it is a difficult situation for any writer to negotiate, and one which highlights the paradox inherent in the way the writer is accorded high artistic status, alongside institutional powerlessness. But even where men are relatively powerless, they are at least expected to exist; a male playwright is unlikely to be reacted to simply on the grounds of his gender, whereas a woman is likely to meet with suspicion, fear or ignorance because she is simply not expected to come into the process at that high level of artistic status.

If a woman argues or explains or defends her work, she is likely to be gossiped about as 'difficult', where if a man does the same he is likely to be seen as strong- minded. Temperament in men may be seen as a nuisance, but it is also seen as a sign of the sensitivity of the artist; in women it is seen as mere emotionality, and like anger or argument is disconcerting since they are simply not meant to be a part of the baggage of feminine behaviour to which all women are expected to conform at some level. Perhaps this is one of the reasons why women tend to fight shy of such public exposure. Women write a great many radio plays – where the production process itself is rather more sheltered. Contact with the producer usually happens over a long period of time, and during the recording the writer remains in the control cubicle, never in direct open contact with the rehearsal and recording process, except through the producer.

Women's reluctance to enter the most public arena as writers may also be related to the nature of the play as a literary form. As an artistic form, the language of a play is entirely social; consisting of speech and (if there are any) stage directions which control the action. A woman writer exploring her literary voice does so in three ways in the theatre. First, like any writer, she will develop her own concerns and her own fictional voice. Second, she can discover her voice only through the voices of others – since even the most contemplative moment or soliloquy in a play is a vocal act of communication between performer and audience. All plays are about some kind of active social relationship between people, even the simplest play in which little appears to 'happen'. Some form of conflict and resolution, even in its most subtle form, is present in every play, in a way it need not be in the novel or in a poem. A playwright makes other people speak and act, exerting a kind of control which is very rare indeed for women in other parts of society.

Of course women are no strangers to dialogue, to power, to emotional interaction, to conflict, to major events. But women's relationship to such things operates largely behind closed doors, in the privacy of the home or in relationships between individuals, rather than in public, among groups of people. The cultural roots of women's experiences are concealed or undervalued, and are rarely those of social and political power, only occasionally those of struggle and visible social change. It is thus not surprising that women have rarely contributed to the drama of great social moment (or is it that they have contributed, but that their perspective has not been understood?), or at any rate are not a full part of the dominant traditions of epic drama, either classical or socialist.

A woman playwright is helping to find a voice in a third sense. Whether she sees herself as a feminist or not, she is bound to be heard, assessed and judged as part of a new set of theatrical voices, which may often be raw, unfamiliar, inexperienced, while they are also vivid, funny, deeply felt and perhaps formally experimental. She will inevitably be contributing material to the current debates on the relationship between gender and fiction. Each play by a woman helps to answer a whole range of questions: can the imagination alone empathise with different, and sometimes alien, emotions and experiences? In a society where men and women are brought up with at worst ignorance, at best prejudice, about the opposite sex, can women accept a status quo in which men claim to speak for them in their culture? Do women write better about women than they do about men? Do men write better about men than they do about women? How do the subjects women choose differ from those chosen by men? How has feminism affected the perceptions of men and women playwrights? How do plays by women affect audiences' assumptions and responses?

****

The four plays in this book have helped provoke some of these questions. I first thought of doing an anthology about four years ago, in 1977, when the most recent wave of plays by women writers really started. At the time I couldn't find a publisher interested – the work was new, unfamiliar, and while it was clear to me from the theatres and companies whose work I knew, that there was a demand and a need for plays by women, it was hard to convince anyone outside those circles. Fortunately things are beginning to change. More and more theatres are taking steps (small and cautious, but steps nevertheless) to find and commission women writers. The feminist groups have provided many opportunities for women writers to have their plays done, and learn by doing. More women are becoming directors, and actively seeking out women playwrights whose work they want to do. And a new, younger generation of women is beginning to enter the theatre with some of the confidence born out of the changes in the last decade. Louise Page, whose *Tissue* is part of this book, sees herself as growing into adulthood post-'68, and in a different climate from the rest of us. In that sense we straddle generations – Caryl Churchill and Pam Gems were writing plays before 1968, whereas I didn't start until 1969.

We represent interestingly different theatrical influences; Caryl Churchill's precise and assured style in her earlier plays then encountered the new ways of collaborative working with theatre groups in the 1970s, which, as she describes, changed her way of seeing her writing and her subject matter. Pam Gems began to write seriously for the theatre with the support and interest of the early 1970s feminism. I began writing plays just before the Women's Liberation Movement started, because I wanted to get back to working in the theatre, and inevitably the debates and excitements of feminism then influenced what I wrote about. As writers we have all written both in isolation, and in collaboration; we all, in different ways and degrees, write about women – though by no means only about women – and we all do so critically and with an urgent concern for women's experiences.

I saw all these plays in their first productions. I found all of them gripping and controversial at the time. The taboos on aspects of female sexuality are particularly vividly explored in both *Tissue* and *Vinegar Tom*, and I can think of no male writer who would have been able to take such empathetic risks. The plays also demonstrate the range of historical subject matter available to women writers – past and present. *Vinegar Tom* is a history play with a difference, a kind of running sub-text to its companion play which Caryl Churchill wrote for Joint Stock – *Light Shining in Buckinghamshire.* It charts the persecution of women in the name of witchcraft – and in its 'modern' songs challenges the audience to examine its own attitudes to women and sexuality.

Aurora charts the nineteenth-century struggles of women for independence, but also is about women's place in culture, in 'high' art, in verse drama. Both *Tissue* and *Dusa* are plays about contemporary survival, and both have a fluid, urgent pace to them, which perhaps derives from the sense of urgency of their writers – even though *Dusa* is more realistic than the darting, daring time-chopping structure of *Tissue*. Three of the plays have men in them, but in all the women are the central protagonists, the main explorers of their own dilemmas, relationships and destinies. This is a rare thing still in contemporary drama.

Implicitly, therefore, the plays challenge the predominant assumptions about our theatre. Clearly women can write history plays, but when those plays deal with female experience, they simply cannot be situated on the battlefield, since women were not on the battlefield. Not in public, anyway. It is virtually impossible to approach a play about women without in some way dealing with female sexuality – and while *Tissue* and *Vinegar Tom* do so explicitly, the other plays do so implicitly. In writing a play about breast cancer Louise Page had to deal with dominant definitions of femininity, in order to probe the pain in the problem; *Vinegar Tom* shows how fear of female sexuality is one of the motor forces behind the witchhunts. *Dusa* presents the difficulty of transforming sexual relationships alongside the dilemmas of motherhood; and *Aurora* implies a sexual independence alongside artistic, economic and maternal independence.

My final choice of plays was partly dictated by the length of the book, but even if the book could have been longer, these plays would have been included. It is not just that I think they are all very good plays but also because they have all continued to have an extended performance life; in other stage productions, on radio, abroad. *Vinegar Tom* was first published by Theatre Quarterly, but went out of print when their play publishing programme folded; it has been performed in this country and in America. *Dusa* has been published by Samuel French's for the amateur market, and it ran successfully in the West End, and has since been done at other theatres round the country. *Tissue* and *Aurora* have both been done on the radio. All four plays started as small-scale fringe productions, initiated out of enthusiasm and commitment, performed in the kind of venues which are often scathingly referred to as places where plays 'preach to the converted'.

Inevitably when new elements appear in theatre work they are greeted with suspicion, misunderstanding, or puzzled ignorance. It is deeply ironic that plays about half the population have been greeted in this way. Perhaps this volume goes some way to proving that there is a lot more to be said about that half of the population; I hope the book will encourage more women to write plays. I hope also that it will demonstrate that women's writing does not need special pleading or apologies, particularly where it is challenging and tough. But I hope that it will also demonstrate that for women to become more publicly visible as playwrights, active efforts are needed in all areas of the theatre industry to change the way women are seen as workers, and represented onstage in plays. In the past, theatrical history seems to have successfully put plays by women to one side. I hope that will not happen to this generation of women writers.

Michelene Wandor

VINEGAR TOM

Vinegar Tom was written for Monstrous Regiment and was first presented at the Humberside Theatre, Hull, on 12 October 1976 with the following cast:

JOAN	Mary McCusker
SUSAN	Sue Todd
ALICE	Gillian Hanna
GOODY	Helen Glavin
BETTY	Josefina Cupido
MARGERY	Linda Broughton
ELLEN	Chris Bowler
JACK	Ian Blower
MAN	
DOCTOR	Roger Allam
BELLRINGER	
PACKER	
KRAMER and SPENCER	Chris Bowler and Mary McCusker

Directed by Pam Brighton
Designed by Andrea Montag
Music by Helen Glavin

Scene One

MAN: Am I the devil?

ALICE: What, sweet?

MAN: I'm the devil. Man in black, they say, they always say, a man in black met me in the night, took me into the thicket and made me commit uncleanness unspeakable.

ALICE: I've seen men in black that's no devils unless clergy and gentlemen are devils.

MAN: Have I not got great burning eyes then?

ALICE: Bright enough eyes.

MAN: Is my body not rough and hairy?

ALICE: I don't like a man too smooth.

MAN: Am I not ice cold?

ALICE: In a ditch in November.

MAN: Didn't I lie on you so heavy I took your breath? Didn't the enormous size of me terrify you?

ALICE: It seemed a fair size like other men's.

MAN: Didn't it hurt you? Are you saying I didn't hurt you?

ALICE: You don't need be the devil, I been hurt by men. Let me go now, you're hurting my shoulder.

MAN: What it is, you didn't see my feet.

ALICE: You never took off your shoes. Take off your shoes if your feet's cloven.

MAN: If you come with me and give me body and soul, you'll never want in this world.

ALICE: Are you saying that as a man?

MAN: Am I saying it as the devil?

ALICE: If you're saying it as a man I'll go with you. There's no one round here knows me going to marry me. There's no way I'll get money. I've a child, mind, I'll not leave the child.

MAN: Has it a father?

ALICE: No, never had.

MAN: So you think that was no sin we did?

ALICE: If it was I don't care.

MAN: Don't say that.

ALICE: You'd say worse living here. Any time I'm happy someone says it's a sin.

MAN: There's some in London say there's no sin. Each man has his own religion nearly, or none at all, and there's women speak out too. They smoke and curse in the tavern and they say flesh is no sin for they are God themselves and can't sin. The men and women lie together and say that's bliss and that's heaven and that's no sin. I believe it for there's such changes.

ALICE: I'd like to go to London and hear them.

MAN: But then I believe with Calvin that few are saved and I am damned utterly. Then I think if I'm damned anyway I might as well sin to make it worthwhile. But I'm afraid to die. I'm afraid of the torture after. One of my family was burnt for a Catholic and they all changed to Protestant and one burnt for that too. I wish I was a Catholic and could confess my sins and burn them away in candles. I believe it all in turn and all at once.

ALICE: Would you take me to London? I've nothing to keep me here except my mother and I'd leave her.

MAN: You don't think I'm sent you by the devil? Sometimes I think the devil has me. And then I think there is no devil. And then I think the devil would make me think there was no devil.

ALICE: I'll never get away from here if you don't take me.

MAN: Will you do everything I say, like a witch with the devil her master?

ALICE: I'll do like a wife with a husband her master and that's enough for man or devil.

MAN: Will you kiss my arse like the devil makes his witches?

ALICE: I'll do what gives us pleasure. Was I good just now?

MAN: In Scotland I saw a witch burnt.

ALICE: Did you? A real witch? Was she a real one?

MAN: She was really burnt for one.

ALICE: Did the spirits fly out of her like black bats? Did the devil make the sky go dark? I've heard plenty tales of witches and I've heard some called witch, there's one in the next village some say and others say not, but she's nothing to see. Did she fly at night on a stick? Did you see her flying?

MAN: I saw her burnt.

ALICE: Tell then. What did she say?

MAN: She couldn't speak, I think. They'd been questioning her. There's wrenching the head with a cord. She came to the stake in a cart and men lifted her out, and the stake held her up when she was tied. She'd been in the boots you see that break the bones.

ALICE: And wood was put round? And a fire lit just like lighting a fire? Oh, I'd have shrieked, I cry the least thing.

MAN: She did shriek.

ALICE: I long to see that. But I might hide my face. Did you hide your face?

MAN: No, I saw it.

ALICE: Did you like seeing it then?

MAN: I may have done.

ALICE: Will you take me with you, to London, to Scotland? Nothing happens here.

MAN: Take you with me?

ALICE: Please, I'd be no trouble . . .

MAN: A whore? Take a whore with me?

ALICE: I'm not that.

MAN: What are you then? What name would you put to yourself? You're not a wife or a widow. You're not a virgin. Tell me a name for what you are.

ALICE: You're not going? Stay a bit.

MAN: I've stayed too long. I'm cold. The devil's cold. Back to my warm fire, eh?

ALICE: Stay with me!

MAN: Get away, will you.

ALICE: Please.

MAN: Get away.

He pushes her and she falls.

ALICE: Go to hell then, go to the devil, you devil.

MAN: Cursing is it? I can outcurse you.

ALICE: You foul devil, you fool, bastard, damn you, you devil!

MAN: Devil take you, whore, whore, damned strumpet, succubus, witch!

ALICE: But come back. I'll not curse you. Don't you curse. We were friends just now.

MAN: You should have behaved better.

ALICE: Will I see you again?

MAN: Unless I see you first.

ALICE: But will I see you? How can I find you?

MAN: You can call on me.

ALICE: How? Where? How shall I call on you?

MAN: You know how to curse. Just call on the devil.

ALICE: Don't tease me, you're not the devil, what's your name?

MAN: Lucifer, isn't it, and Beelzebub.

ALICE: No, what's your name?

MAN: Darling was my name, and sweeting, till you called me devil.

ALICE: I'll not call you devil, come back, what's your name?

MAN: You won't need to know it. You won't be seeing me.

Scene Two

JACK: The river meadow is the one to get.

MARGERY: I thought the long field up the hill.

JACK: No, the river meadow for the cattle.

MARGERY: But Jack, for corn. Think of the long field full of wheat.

JACK: He's had a bad crop two years. That's why he can't pay the rent.

MARGERY: No, but he's got no cattle. We'd be all right.

JACK: If we took both fields.

MARGERY: Could we? Both?

JACK: The more we have the more we can afford.

MARGERY: And we'll pray God sends us sunshine.

JACK: Who's that down by the river?

MARGERY: That Alice, is it, wandering about?

JACK: I'm surprised Mother Noakes can pay her rent.

MARGERY: Just a cottage isn't much.

JACK: I've been wondering if we'll see them turned out.

MARGERY: I don't know why she's let stay. If we all lived like her it wouldn't be the fine estate it is. And Alice . . .

JACK: You can't blame Alice.

MARGERY: You can blame her. You can't be surprised. She's just what I'd expect of a girl brought up by Joan Noakes.

JACK: If we rent both fields, we'll have to hire a man to help with the harvest.

MARGERY: Hire a man?

JACK: That's not Alice.

MARGERY: It's not Miss Betty out by herself again?

JACK: I wouldn't be her father, not even to own the land.

MARGERY: That's a fine idea, hire a man.

JACK: She's coming here.

MARGERY: What we going to do?

JACK: Be respectful.

MARGERY: No, but shall we take her home? She's not meant to. She's still shut up in her room, everyone says.

JACK: I won't be sorry to see her.

MARGERY: I love to see her. She was always so soft on your lap, not like ours all hard edges. I could sit all afternoon just to smell her hair. But she's not a child, now, you can have run in and out and touch her. She's in trouble at home and we shouldn't help her do wrong.

JACK: We can't stop her, can we, if she walks in?

They wait and in a moment BETTY *does come in.*

MARGERY: Miss Betty, how nice.

BETTY: I came to see you milking the cows.

JACK: We finished milking, miss. The cows are in.

BETTY: Is it that late?

MARGERY: You want to get home before dark.

BETTY: No, I don't. I want to be out in the dark. It's not late, it's dark in the day time. I could stay out for hours if it was summer.

JACK: If you want to come and see the farm, Miss Betty, you should ask your father to bring you one morning when he's inspecting the estate.

BETTY: I'm not let go where I like.

JACK: I've business with your father.

MARGERY: We're going to take on the river meadow for the cattle.

JACK: And the long field up the hill.

BETTY: I used to play here all day. Nothing's different. Have you still got Betty's mug?

MARGERY: That's right, she had her special mug.

BETTY: I milked the red cow right into it one day. I got milk in my eye.

JACK: She died, that red cow. But we've four new cows you've not seen.

MARGERY: Died last week. There's two or three cows died in the neighbourhood.

BETTY: I wish she hadn't.

JACK: That don't matter, losing one, we're doing well enough.

MARGERY: And you're doing well, I hear, miss.

BETTY: What?

MARGERY: I hear you're leaving us for better things.

BETTY: No.

MARGERY: I was only saying yesterday, our little Miss Betty that was and now to be a lady with her own house and . . .

BETTY: They lock me up. I said I won't marry him so they lock me up. Don't you know that?

MARGERY: I had heard something.

BETTY: I get out the window.

MARGERY: Hadn't you better have him, Betty, and be happy? Everyone hopes so. Everyone loves a wedding.

BETTY: Margery, can I stay here tonight?

MARGERY: They'd worry for you.

BETTY: Can I? Please?

JACK: There's no bed fit for you, miss.

BETTY: On my way here I climbed a tree. I could see the whole estate. I could see the other side of the river. I wanted to jump off. And fly.

MARGERY: Shall Jack walk home with you, miss, now it's getting dark?

Scene Three

JOAN: Alice?

ALICE: No need wake up, mum.

JOAN: You'll catch cold out all night in this weather.

ALICE: Don't wake up if it's only to moan at me.

JOAN: Who were you with?

ALICE: Did he wake up?

JOAN: No, not a sound.

ALICE: He's sleeping better. Not so much bad dreams.

JOAN: Come on, child, there's some broth left.

ALICE: I couldn't eat.

JOAN: You stay out half the night, you don't even enjoy it. You stay in with the boy. You sit by the fire with no one to talk to but old Vinegar Tomcat. I'll go out.

ALICE: You go out?

JOAN: Funny, isn't it? What would I do going out?

ALICE: I'll stay in if you like.

JOAN: Where would I go? Who wants an old woman?

ALICE: You want me to stay with you more?

JOAN: An old woman wandering about in the cold.

ALICE: Do you want some broth, mum?

JOAN: Who were you with this time? Anyone I know?

ALICE: Oh mum, I'm sick of myself.

JOAN: If we'd each got a man we'd be better off.

ALICE: You weren't better off, mum. You've told me often you're glad he's dead. Think how he used to beat you.

JOAN: We'd have more to eat, that's one thing.

Nobody Sings

I met an old old woman
Who made my blood run cold.
You don't stop wanting sex, she said,
Just because you're old.
>> Oh nobody sings about it,
>> but it happens all the time.

I could be glad of the change of life,
But it makes me feel so strange.
If your life is being wanted
Do you want your life to change?
>> Oh nobody sings about it,
>> but it happens all the time.

Do you want your skin to wrinkle
And your cunt get sore and dry?
And they say it's just your hormones
If you cry and cry and cry.
>> Oh nobody sings about it,
>> but it happens all the time.

Nobody ever saw me,
She whispered in a rage.
They were blinded by my beauty, now
They're blinded by my age.
>> Oh nobody sings about it,
>> but it happens all the time.

Scene Four

MARGERY *is churning*.

JACK: Hurry up with that butter, woman.

MARGERY: Butter won't come.

JACK: There's other work to do.

MARGERY: Butter won't come.

JACK: You don't churn. You sit gossiping.

MARGERY: Who would I talk to?

JACK: I heard your voice now.

MARGERY: Mother Noakes.

JACK: Always hanging about.

MARGERY: Her girl's no better.

JACK: Was her girl here? No.

MARGERY: I told her be on her way. Mother Noakes.

JACK: You tell her.

MARGERY: I told her.

JACK: Get on now with the butter and don't be always gossiping.

JACK goes. MARGERY churns and sings very quietly.

MARGERY: Come butter come, come butter come. Johnny's standing at the gate waiting for a butter cake. Come butter come, come butter come. Johnny's standing at the gate waiting for a butter cake. Come butter come, come butter come. Johnny's standing at the gate . . .

She stops as she realises JOAN NOAKES has come in and is standing behind her.

JOAN: Just passing by.

MARGERY: Again.

JOAN: I wonder could you lend me a little yeast? I've no yeast, see. I'm fresh out of yeast. I've no bread in the house and I thought, I thought . . . I'll do a little baking now and brew a little beer maybe . . . and I went to get some yeast and I've no yeast. Who'd have thought it? No yeast at all.

MARGERY: You'd be better without beer.

JOAN: I thought a little yeast as I was passing.

MARGERY: You get drunk. You should be ashamed.

JOAN: To bake a couple of little small loaves.

MARGERY: I've no yeast.

JOAN: A couple of little small loaves wouldn't take much yeast. A woman comfortable off with a fine man and a nice field and five cows and three pigs and plenty of apples that makes a good cider, bless you, Margery, many's the time . . .

you'd not grudge a neighbour a little loaf? Many's the good times, eh, Margery? I've my own flour, you know, I'm not asking for flour.

MARGERY: I gave you yeast last week.

JOAN: A little small crumb of yeast and God will bless you for kindness to your poor old neighbour.

MARGERY: You're not so badly off, Joan Noakes. You're not on the parish.

JOAN: If I was I'd be fed. I should be on relief, then I'd not trouble you. There's some on relief, better off than me. I get nothing.

MARGERY: What money you get you drink.

JOAN: If you'd my troubles, Margery, you'd be glad of a drink, but as you haven't, thank God, and lend me a little yeast like a good woman.

MARGERY: I've no yeast.

JOAN: I know you, Margery.

MARGERY: What do you know?

JOAN: I know you've got yeast. My eyes are old, but I see through you. You're a cold woman and getting worse and you'll die without a friend in this parish when if you gave yeast to your good neighbours everyone would bless you . . .

MARGERY: I've no yeast.

JOAN: But you don't give and they say what a mean bitter woman and curse you.

MARGERY: There's nobody curses me. Now get out of my dairy. Dirty old woman you are, smelling of drink, come in here day after day begging, and stealing, too, I shouldn't wonder . . .

JOAN: You shouldn't say that.

MARGERY: . . . and your great ugly cat in here stealing the cream. Get out of my dairy.

JOAN: You'll be sorry you spoke to me like that. I've always been your friend, Margery, but now you'll find I'm not.

MARGERY: I've work to do. Now get out. I'm making my butter.

JOAN: Damn your butter to hell.

MARGERY: Will you get out?

JOAN: Devil take you and your man and your fields and your cows and your butter and your yeast and your beer and your bread and your cider and your cold face . . .

MARGERY: Will you go?

JOAN *goes*. MARGERY *churns*.

MARGERY: Come butter come, come butter come. Johnny's standing at the gate waiting for a butter cake. Come butter . . . It's not coming, this butter. I'm sick of it.

JACK *comes*.

JACK: What's all this? You're a lazy woman, you know that? Times are bad enough. The little black calf don't look well.

MARGERY: Butter won't come. Mother Noakes said damn the butter to hell.

JACK: Lazy slut, get on with it.

MARGERY: Come butter come. Come butter come. Come butter come. Come butter come. Come butter come. Come butter . . . Mother Noakes come begging and borrowing. She still got my big bowl I give her some eggs in that time she was poorly. She makes out I've treated her bad. I've been a good neighbour to that woman years out of mind and no return. We'll get that bowl back off her. Jack, do you hear me? Go over Mother Noakes and get my bowl. And we'll heat a horseshoe red hot and put it in the milk to make the butter come.

Scene Five

SUSAN: Don't always talk of men.

ALICE: He knew what he was doing.

SUSAN: You'll know what he was doing in a few months.

ALICE: No, it never happens. The cunning woman put a charm inside me.

SUSAN: Take more than a charm to do me good.

ALICE: Not again? Does he know?

SUSAN: He wants it. I know the night it was. He said, 'Let's hope a fine child comes of it.'

ALICE: And what did you say?

SUSAN: Devil take it.

ALICE: What he say to that?

SUSAN: He don't like me swearing.

ALICE: But the baby's not a year.

SUSAN: Two weeks late, so.

ALICE: But the baby's not weaned.

SUSAN: The boy wasn't weaned when I fell for the baby.

ALICE: You could go see the cunning woman.

SUSAN: What for?

ALICE: She's a good midwife.

SUSAN: I don't want a midwife. I got my mother, anyway. I don't want to think about it. Nearly died last time. I was two days.

ALICE: Go and see the cunning woman. Just go see.

SUSAN: What for?

ALICE: She could say for certain.

SUSAN: I'm sure for certain.

ALICE: She could give you a charm.

SUSAN: They do say the pain is what's sent to a woman for her sins. I complained last time after churching, and he said I must think on Eve who brought the sin into the world that got me pregnant. I must think on how woman tempts man, and how she pays God with her pain having the baby. So if we try to get round the pain, we're going against God.

ALICE: I hate my body.

SUSAN: You mustn't say that. God sent his son . . .

ALICE: Blood every month, and no way out of that but to be sick and swell up, and no way out of that but pain. No way out of all that till we're old and that's worse. I can't bear to see my mother if she changes her clothes. If I was a man I'd go to London and Scotland and never come back and take a girl under a bush and on my way.

SUSAN: You could go to the cunning woman.

ALICE: What for?

SUSAN: Charm.

ALICE: What for?

SUSAN: Love charm bring him back.

ALICE: I don't want him back.

SUSAN: Did he look wonderful, more than anyone here, that he's got you so low?

ALICE: It was dark, I wouldn't know him again.

SUSAN: Not so much how he looked as how he felt?

ALICE: I could do with it now, I can tell you. I could do with walking across that field again and finding him there just the same. I want a man I can have when I want, not if I'm lucky to meet some villain one night.

SUSAN: You always say you don't want to be married.

ALICE: I don't want to be married. Look at you. Who'd want to be you?

SUSAN: He doesn't beat me.

ALICE: He doesn't beat you.

SUSAN: What's wrong with me? Better than you.

ALICE: Three babies and what, two, three times miscarried and wonderful he doesn't beat you.

SUSAN: No one's going to marry you because they know you here. That's why you say you don't want to be married – because no one's going to ask you round here, because they know you.

They move apart. JACK *has been lingering in the background a while, and now comes up to* ALICE.

JACK: It's not you I've come to see.

ALICE: Never thought it was.

JACK: You should have done then.

ALICE: Why?

JACK: You know why.

ALICE: You've come to see my mum, have you?

JACK: I've business with her, yes. That's why I came.

ALICE: She's somewhere around. I'll get her.

JACK: No hurry. Wait a bit. Never seem to talk.

ALICE: Nothing to talk about.

JACK: I'm forgetting. I brought something.

He gives her two apples.

ALICE: Thank you. What then?

JACK: Am I not handsome enough, is that it?

ALICE: I don't want trouble.

JACK: No one's to know.

ALICE: If I say you're not handsome enough, will you go away?

JACK: Alice, you must. I have dreams.

ALICE: You've a wife.

JACK: I'm no good to my wife. I can't do it. Not these three months. It's only when I dream of you or like now talking to you . . .

ALICE: Mum. There's someone to see you.

JACK: Alice, have some pity . . .

ALICE: Do you hear me? Mum? She'll be out to see you.

She moves away. JOAN *comes.*

JOAN: What's the matter?

JACK: I've come for the bowl.

JOAN: Bowl? Bowl?

JACK: Bowl my wife gave you some eggs in, you ungrateful old hag.

JOAN: You're asking for the bowl? You think I wouldn't give you back your bowl? You think I'm stealing your bowl? When have I ever kept anything? Have your bowl. I'll get your bowl and much good may it do you.

JACK: Then get it, damn you, and quick or you'll feel my hand.

She goes.

ALICE: Why treat her like that?

JACK: Don't speak to me. Let me get the bowl and go.

ALICE: And don't come back.

JACK: Alice, I'd be good to you. I'm not a poor man. I could give you things for your boy . . .

ALICE: Go away to hell.

JOAN *comes back.*

JOAN: Here's your bowl, Jack, and the devil go with it. Get away home and I hope you've more trouble there than I have here.

JACK: I'll break your neck if you speak to me.

JOAN: You lift your hand to me, may it drop off.

ALICE: Go home away to hell, man.

JACK *goes.*

JOAN: Away to hell with him. Never liked the man. Never liked the wife.

ALICE: Don't think on them, mum. They're not worth your time. Go in by the fire, go on, go in and be warm.

JOAN *goes.* SUSAN *approaches.*

Nobody likes my mother. That's what it is why nobody wants me.

SUSAN: I'm sorry for what I said, Alice.

ALICE: Going to see the cunning woman then?

SUSAN: Are you going for a love charm?

ALICE: It's something to do, isn't it? Better than waiting and waiting for something to happen. If I had a charm I could make him just appear in front of me now, I'd do anything. Will you come?

ALICE *gives* SUSAN *an apple.*

SUSAN: I'll keep you company then. Just tell her my trouble. There's no harm.

Oh Doctor

Oh, doctor, tell
me, make me well.
What's wrong with me
the way I am?
I know I'm sad.
I may be sick.
I may be bad.
Please cure me quick,
oh doctor.

Scene Six

BETTY *tied to a chair. The* DOCTOR *is*

about to bleed her arm.

BETTY: Why am I tied? Tied to be bled. Why am I bled? Because I was screaming. Why was I screaming? Because I'm bad. Why was I bad? Because I was happy. Why was I happy? Because I ran out by myself and got away from them and – Why was I screaming? Because I'm bad. Why am I bad? Because I'm tied. Why am I tied? Because I was happy. Why was I happy? Because I was screaming.

DOCTOR: Hysteria is a woman's weakness. Hysteron, Greek, the womb. Excessive blood causes an imbalance in the humours. The noxious gases that form inwardly every month rise to the brain and cause behaviour quite contrary to the patient's real feelings. After bleeding you must be purged. Tonight you shall be blistered. You will soon be well enough to be married.

Oh Doctor

Where are you taking my skin?
Where are you putting my bones?
I shut my eyes and I opened wide,
But why is my heart on the other side?
Why are you putting my brain in my cunt?
You're putting me back all back to front.

Stop looking up me with your metal eye.
Stop cutting me apart before I die.
Stop, put me back.
Stop, put me back.
Put back my body.

Who are you giving my womb?
Who are you showing my breath?
Tell me what you whisper to nurse,
Whatever I've got, you're making it worse.
I'm wide awake, but I still can't shout.
Why can't I see what you're taking out?

Stop looking up me with your metal eye.
Stop cutting me apart before I die.
Stop, put me back.
Stop, put me back.
Put back my body.

Oh, doctor, tell
me, make me well.
What's wrong with me
the way I am?
I know I'm sad
I may be sick.
I may be bad.
Please cure me quick,
oh doctor,

What's wrong with me the way I am?
What's wrong with me?

I want to see myself.
I want to see inside myself.
Give me back my head.
I'll put my heart in straight.
Let me out of bed now.
I can't wait
To see myself.
Give me back my body.
I can see myself.
Give me back my body.
I can see myself.

Scene Seven

MARGERY: Jack, Jack, come quick – Jack.

JACK: What's the matter now?

MARGERY: The calves. Have you seen the calves?

JACK: What's the woman on about?

MARGERY: The calves are shaking and they've a terrible stench, so you can't go near them and their bellies are swollen up. (JACK *goes off.*) There's no good running. There's nothing you can do for them. They'll die like the red cow. You don't love me. Damn this stinking life to hell. Calves stinking and shaking there. No good you going to see, Jack. Better stand and curse. Everything dying on us. Aah. What's that? Who's there? Get out, you beast, get out. (*She throws her shoe.*) Jack, Jack.

JACK: Hold your noise.

MARGERY: That nasty old cat of Mother Noakes. I'll kill that cat if I get it, stinking up my clean dairy, stealing my cream. Where's it gone?

JACK: Let it go.

MARGERY: What you think of those calves then? Nothing to be done is there? What can we do? Nothing. Nothing to be done. Can't do nothing. Oh. Oh.

JACK: Now what is it?

MARGERY: Jack!

JACK: What is it? Don't frighten me, woman.

MARGERY: My head, oh, my stomach. Oh, Jack, I feel ill.

She sits on the ground.

JACK: Get up, woman. It's no time. There's things to do.

MARGERY: Nothing.

JACK: Lie there a bit then. You'll maybe feel better. I can hardly stir myself. What have I done to deserve it? Why me? Why my calves shaking? Why my wife falling down?

MARGERY: It's passing now.

JACK: Why me?

MARGERY: That was a terrible pain. I still feel it. I'm shaking, look.

JACK: Other people sin and aren't punished so much as we are.

MARGERY: We must pray to God.

JACK: We do pray to God, and he sends afflictions.

MARGERY: It must be we deserve it somehow, but I don't know how. I do my best. I do my best, Jack, God knows, don't I, Jack? God knows I do my best.

JACK: Don't other people sin? Is it just me?

MARGERY: You're not a bad man, Jack.

JACK: I must be the worst man.

MARGERY: No, dear.

JACK: Would God send all this to a good man? Would he? It's my sins those calves shaking and stinking and swelling up their bellies in there.

MARGERY: Don't talk so.

JACK: My sins stinking and swelling up.

MARGERY: Unless it's not God.

JACK: How can I bear it?

MARGERY: If it's not God.

JACK: What?

MARGERY: If it's not God sends the trouble.

JACK: The devil?

MARGERY: One of his servants. If we're bewitched, Jack, that explains all.

JACK: If we're bewitched . . .

MARGERY: Butter not coming. Calves swelling. Me struck in the head.

JACK: Then it's not my sins. Good folk get bewitched.

MARGERY: Good folk like us.

JACK: It can happen to anyone.

MARGERY: Rich folk can have spells against them.

JACK: It's good people the witches want to hurt.

MARGERY: The devil can't bear to see us so good.

JACK: You know who it is?

MARGERY: Who?

JACK: The witch. Who it is.

MARGERY: Who?

JACK: You know who.

MARGERY: She cursed the butter to hell.

JACK: She cursed me when I got the bowl.

MARGERY: She said I'd be sorry I'd spoken to her.

JACK: She wished me trouble at home.

MARGERY: Devil take your man and your cows, she said that, and your butter. She cursed the calves see and she's made them shake. She struck me on the head and in the stomach.

JACK: I'll break her neck.

MARGERY: Be careful now, what she might do.

JACK: I'm not afraid of an old witch.

MARGERY: You should be. She could kill you.

JACK: I'll kill her first.

MARGERY: Wait, Jack. Let's meet cunning with cunning. What we must do is get the spell off.

JACK: She's not going to take it off for asking. She might for a few hard knocks.

MARGERY: No, wait, Jack. We can take the spell off and never go near her. Serve her right.

JACK: What we do then? Burn something?

MARGERY: Burn an animal alive, don't we? Or bury it alive. That takes witchcraft off the rest.

JACK: Burn the black calf then shall we? We'll get some straw and wood and put it in the yard and the calf on top and set it on fire.

MARGERY: Will it walk?

JACK: Or I'll carry it.

MARGERY: It stinks terrible.

JACK: Stink of witchcraft it is. Burn it up.

MARGERY: We must pray to God to keep us safe from the devil. Praying's strong against witches.

JACK: We'll pray God help us and help ourselves too.

MARGERY: She'll see the fire and smell it and she'll know we're fighting her back, stinking old witch, can't hurt us.

Something to Burn

What can we do, there's nothing to do,
about sickness and hunger and dying.
What can we do, there's nothing to do,
nothing but cursing and crying.
> Find something to burn.
> Let it go up in smoke.
> Burn your troubles away.

Sometimes it's witches, or what will you choose?
Sometimes it's lunatics, shut them away.
It's blacks and it's women and often it's Jews.
We'd all be quite happy if they'd go away.
> Find something to burn.
> Let it go up in smoke.
> Burn your troubles away.

Scene Eight

ELLEN: Take it or leave it, my dear, it's one to me. If you want to be rid of your trouble, you'll take it. But only you know what you want.

SUSAN: It's not what I came for.

ALICE: Of course it is.

SUSAN: I wanted to know for certain.

ALICE: You know for certain.

SUSAN: I want a charm against pain.

ELLEN: I'll come as your midwife if you

send for me near the time and do what I can, if that's all you want.

ALICE: She wants to be rid of it. Well, do you want it?

SUSAN: I don't want it but I don't want to be rid of it. I want to be rid of it, but not do anything to be rid of it.

ELLEN: If you won't do anything to help yourself you must stay as you are.

SUSAN: I shall pray to God.

ALICE: It's no sin. You just give yourself the drink.

SUSAN: Oh, I don't know.

ELLEN: Let her go home. She can come back. You have your charm safe, Alice? I could do more if you could come at the young man and give him a potion I'd let you have.

ALICE: If I could come at him he wouldn't need potion.

ELLEN: And you're sure you've nothing of his?

ALICE: He gave me nothing.

ELLEN: A few hairs or a drop of blood makes all the difference. It's part of him and the powers can work on it to call him.

ALICE: I'll pull a few hairs out next time I've a lover. Come on, Susan.

ELLEN: For your heartache I'll give you these herbs to boil up in water and drink at night. Give you a sound sleep and think less of him.

ALICE: Don't want to think less of him.

ELLEN: You have your sleep. There'll be other men along if not that one. Clever girl like you could think of other things.

ALICE: Like what?

ELLEN: Learn a trade.

ALICE: Nothing dangerous.

ELLEN: Where's the danger in herbs?

ALICE: Not just herbs.

ELLEN: Where's the danger in healing?

ALICE: Not just healing, is it?

ELLEN: There's powers, and you use them for healing or hurt. You use them how you like. There's no hurt if you're healing so where's the danger? You could use them. Not everyone can.

ALICE: Learn the herbs?

ELLEN: There's all kinds of wisdom. Bit by bit I'd teach you.

ALICE: I'd never thought.

ELLEN: There's no hurry. I don't want you unless it's what you want. You'll be coming by to leave a little something for me in a few days, since I have to live and wouldn't charge you. You can tell me how you've got on with your young man and what you're thinking.

ALICE: Yes, I'll be coming by. Goodnight then. What are you standing there for, Susan?

SUSAN: Maybe I'll take some potion with me. And see when I get home whether I take it.

ELLEN: Don't be afraid if it makes you very sick. It's to do you good.

Scene Nine

BETTY: I don't know what I'm here for. I've had so much treatment already. The doctor comes every day.

ELLEN: You know what you're here for.

BETTY: The doctor says people like you don't know anything. He thinks he's cured me because I said I would get married to stop them locking me up. But I'll never do it.

ELLEN: Do you want a potion to make you love the man?

BETTY: I'd rather have one to make him hate me so he'd leave me alone. Or make him die.

ELLEN: The best I can do for you is help you sleep. I won't harm him for you, so don't ask. Get some sleep and think out what you want.

BETTY: Can I come again sometimes just to be here? I like it here.

ELLEN: Come when you like. I don't charge but you'll bring a little present.

BETTY: I'll give you anything if you can help me.

ELLEN: Come when you like.

Scene Ten

ELLEN: I'm not saying I can't do anything. But if I can't, it's because you've left it too late.

JACK: Lift your hand to me, she said, may it drop off. Then next day it went stiff.

MARGERY: We want to be certain. I've talked to others and they've things against her too. She's cursed and scolded two or three, and one's lame and the other lost her hen. And while we were talking we thought of her great cat that's always in my dairy, stinking it up and stealing the cream. Ah what's that, I said crying out, didn't I, and that was the cat, and I was struck down with a blow inside my head. That's her familiar sent her by Satan.

JACK: I've seen a rat run out of her yard into ours and I went for it with a pitchfork and the spikes were turned aside and nearly went in my own foot by her foul magic. And that rat's another of her imps.

MARGERY: But you don't like to think it of your neighbour. Time was she was neighbourly enough. If you could tell us it was true, we could act against her more certain in our minds.

JACK: I shouted at her over the fence, I said I'll have you hanged you old strumpet, burnt and hanged, and she cursed me again.

MARGERY: We burnt a calf alive to save our calves but it was too late. If I knew for certain it was her I'd be easier.

ELLEN: I've a glass here, a cloudy glass. Look in the glass, so, and see if any face comes into it.

She gives them a mirror.

MARGERY: Come on, Jack, don't be afraid.

JACK: I don't like it.

MARGERY: Come on, it's good magic to find a witch.

ELLEN: Look in the glass and think on all the misfortunes you've had and see what comes.

MARGERY: Nothing yet. Do you see anything?

JACK: No.

MARGERY: Nothing still.

JACK: Don't keep talking.

MARGERY: Look.

JACK: What?

MARGERY: Did something move in the glass? My heart's beating so.

JACK: It's too dark.

MARGERY: No. Look.

JACK: I did see something.

MARGERY: It's the witch.

JACK: It's her sure enough.

MARGERY: It is, isn't it, Jack? Mother Noakes, isn't it?

JACK: It was Mother Noakes in that glass.

ELLEN: There then. You have what you came for.

MARGERY: Proves she's a witch then?

ELLEN: Not for me to say one's a witch or not a witch. I give you the glass and you see in it what you see in it.

JACK: Saw Mother Noakes.

MARGERY: Proves she's a witch.

ELLEN: Saw what you come to see. Is your mind easy?

Scene Eleven

JACK: Want to ask you something private. It's about my . . . (*He gestures, embarrassed.*) It's gone. I can't do anything with it, haven't for some time. I accepted that. But now it's not even there, it's completely gone. There's a girl bewitched me. She's daughter of that witch. And I've heard how witches sometimes get a whole boxful and they move and stir by themselves like living creatures and the witch feeds them oats and hay. There was one witch told a man in my condition to climb a tree and he'd find a nest with several in it and take which he liked, and when he took the big one she said no, not that one, because that one belongs to the parish priest. I don't want a big one, I want my own back, and this witch has it.

ELLEN: You'd better go and ask her nicely for it.

JACK: Is that all you can say? Can't you force her to give it me?

ELLEN: It's sure to come back. You ask the girl nicely, she'll give it you back. I'll give you a little potion to take.

JACK: Kill her else.

Scene Twelve

JOAN: That's a foul stink. I don't know how you can stay there. Whatever is it?

MARGERY: Do you know why you've come?

JOAN: I was passing.

MARGERY: Why were you passing?

JOAN: Can't I pass by your door now? Time was it was always open for me.

MARGERY: And what's that?

JOAN: A foul stink. Whatever are you making? I thought I'd come and see you as I was passing. I don't want any trouble between us. I thought, come and see her, make it all right.

MARGERY: You come to see me because of that. That's my piss boiling. And two feathers of your chicken burning. It's a foul stink brings a witch. If you come when I do that, proves you've a spell on me. And now I'll get it off. You know how?

JOAN: Come and see you. Make it all right.

MARGERY: Blood you, that's how.

MARGERY *scratches* JOAN's *head.*

JOAN: Damn you, get away.

MARGERY: Can't hurt me now. And if that doesn't bring the spell off I'll burn your thatch.

If Everybody Worked as Hard as Me

If everybody worked as hard as me,
if our children's shirts are white,
if their language is polite,
if nobody stays out late at night,
Oh, happy family.
Oh, the country's what it is because
the family's what it is because
the wife is what she is
to her man.
Oh I do all I can.

Yes, I do all I can.
I try to do what's right,
so I'll never be alone and afraid in the night.
And nobody comes knocking at my door in
the night.
The horrors that are done will not be done
to me.

Nobody loves a scold,
nobody loves a slut,
nobody loves you when you're old,
unless you're someone's gran.
Nobody loves you
unless you keep your mouth shut.
Nobody loves you
if you don't support your man.
Oh you can,
oh you can
have a happy family.

If everybody worked as hard as me,
sometimes you'll be bored,
you'll often be ignored,
but in your heart you'll know you are
adored.
Oh, happy family.
Your dreams will all come true.
You'll make your country strong.
Oh the country's what it is because
the family's what it is because
the wife is what she is
to her man.
Oh please do all you can.
Yes, please do all you can
Oh, please don't do what's wrong,
so you'll never be alone and afraid in the
night.
So nobody comes knocking at your door in
the night.
So the horrors that are done will not be done
to you.

Yes you can.
Yes you can.
Oh the country's what it is because
the family's what it is because
the wife is what she is
to her man.

Scene Thirteen

SUSAN: You're sure it was him? You said you wouldn't know him.

ALICE: I did when I saw him.

SUSAN: Riding? Couldn't see him close.

ALICE: Close enough to be spattered with

his mud. He saw me.

SUSAN: But he didn't show he knew you.

ALICE: Pretended not to.

SUSAN: It wasn't him.

ALICE: It was him.

SUSAN: And you don't know the beautiful lady?

ALICE: I'll know her again. Scratch her eyes if I come at her.

SUSAN: What was she wearing?

ALICE: What was she wearing? How should I know? A fine rich dress made her beautiful, I suppose. Are you trying to plague me?

SUSAN: Was he in black still?

ALICE: Blue velvet jacket.

SUSAN: Blue velvet.

ALICE: Yes, damn you, I said that before. Are you stupid? (*Silence.*) For God's sake, now what is it? Are you crying? Shouldn't I be crying?

SUSAN: It's not your fault, Ally. I cry all the time.

ALICE: You're still weak, that's what it is. It's the blood you lost. You should rest more.

SUSAN: I don't want him to know.

ALICE: Doesn't he know?

SUSAN: He may guess but I don't dare ask. He was out all day that day and I said I'd been ill, but not why.

ALICE: It's done anyway.

SUSAN: Can't be undone.

ALICE: You're not sorry now?

SUSAN: I don't know.

ALICE: You'd be a fool to be sorry.

SUSAN: I am sorry. I'm wicked. You're wicked.

She cries.

ALICE: Oh, Susan, you're tired out, that's all. You're not wicked. You'd have cried more to have it. All the extra work, another baby.

SUSAN: I like babies.

ALICE: You'll have plenty more, God, you'll have plenty. What's the use of crying?

SUSAN: You were crying for that lover.

ALICE: I'm not now. I'd sooner kill him. If I could get at him. If thoughts could get at him he'd feel it.

SUSAN: I'm so tired, Ally.

ALICE: Do you think it's true thoughts can reach someone?

SUSAN: What are you thinking of?

ALICE: Like if I had something of his, I could bring him. Or harm him.

SUSAN: Don't try that.

ALICE: But I've nothing of his. I'd have to make a puppet.

SUSAN: Don't talk so. Oh, don't, Alice, when I'm so tired.

ALICE: Does it have to be like? Is it like just if you say it's like?

SUSAN: Alice!

ALICE: If I get this wet mud, it's like clay. There should be at least a spider or some ashes of bones, but mud will do. Here's a man's shape, see, that's his head and that's arms and legs.

SUSAN: I'm going home. I'm too tired to move.

ALICE: You stay here and watch. This is the man. We know who though we don't know his name. Now here's a pin, let's prick him. Where shall I prick him? Between the legs first so he can't get on with his lady.

SUSAN: Alice, stop.

ALICE: Once in the head to drive him mad. Shall I give him one in the heart? Do I want him to die yet? Or just waste till I please.

SUSAN: Alice . . .

SUSAN *tries to get the mud man, it falls on the ground and breaks.*

ALICE: Now look. You've broken him up. You've killed him.

SUSAN: I haven't.

ALICE: All in pieces. Think of the poor man. Come apart.

SUSAN: I didn't. Alice, I didn't. It was you.

ALICE: If it was me, I don't care.

SUSAN: Alice, what have you done? Oh Alice, Alice.

ALICE: It's not true, stupid. It's not him.

SUSAN: How do you know?

ALICE: It's a bit of mud.

SUSAN: But you said.

ALICE: That's just words.

SUSAN: But . . .

ALICE: No. I did nothing. I never do anything. Might be better if I did. (*They sit in silence.*) You're crying again. Here, don't cry.

ALICE *holds* SUSAN *while she cries.*

SUSAN: Little clay puppet like a tiny baby not big enough to live and we crumble it away.

JACK *comes.*

JACK: Witch.

ALICE: Are you drunk?

JACK: Give it back.

ALICE: What?

JACK: Give it back.

ALICE: What now, Jack?

JACK: Give it me back. You know. You took it from me these three months. I've not been a man since. You bewitched me. You took it off me.

ALICE: Is he mad?

SUSAN: What is it?

ALICE: Susan's ill, will you leave us alone?

JACK: Everyone comes near you is ill. Give it back, come on, give it back.

ALICE: How can I?

JACK: She said speak nicely to you. I would, Alice, if you were good to me. I never wanted this. Please, sweet good Alice, give it back.

ALICE: What? How can I?

JACK: Give it me.

He grabs her round the neck. SUSAN *screams.*

ALICE: Damn you!

SUSAN: You'll kill her . . .

JACK: Give it me . . .

SUSAN: Let her go, she'll give it you whatever it is, you'll kill her Jack.

JACK *lets go.*

JACK: Give it me then. Come on.

SUSAN: Wait, she can't move, leave her alone.

JACK: Give it me.

ALICE *puts her hand between his thighs.*

ALICE: There. It's back.

JACK: It is. It is back. Thank you, Alice. I wasn't sure you were a witch till then.

JACK *goes.*

SUSAN: What you doing Alice? Alice? Alice?

ALICE *turns to her.*

ALICE: It's nothing. He's mad. Oh my neck, Susan. Oh, I'd laugh if it didn't hurt.

SUSAN: Don't touch me. I'll not be touched by a witch.

Scene Fourteen

BELLRINGER: Whereas if anyone has any complaint against any woman for a witch, let them go to the townhall and lay their complaint. For a man is in town that is a famous finder of witches and has had above thirty hanged in the country round and he will discover if they are or no. Whereas if anyone has any complaint against any woman for a witch, let them go . . .

MARGERY: Stopped the butter.

JACK: Killed the calves.

MARGERY: Struck me in the head.

JACK: Lamed my hand.

MARGERY: Struck me in the stomach.

JACK: Bewitched my organ.

MARGERY: When I boiled my urine she came.

JACK: Blooded her and made my hand well.

MARGERY: Burnt her thatch.

JACK: And Susan, her friend, is like possessed screaming and crying and lay two days without speaking.

MARGERY: Susan's baby turned blue and its limbs twisted and it died.

JACK: Boy threw stones and called them witch, and after he vomited pins and straw.

MARGERY: Big nasty cat she has in her bed and sends it to people's dairies.

JACK: A rat's her imp.

MARGERY: And the great storm last night brought a tree down in the lane, who made that out of a clear sky?

PACKER: I thank God that he has brought me again where I am needed. Don't be afraid any more. You have been in great danger but the devil can never overcome the faithful. For God in his mercy has called me and shown me a wonderful way of finding out witches, which is finding the place on the body of the witch made insensitive to pain by the devil. So that if you prick that place with a pin no blood comes out and the witch feels nothing at all.

PACKER *and* GOODY *take* JOAN, *and* GOODY *holds her, while* PACKER *pulls up her skirts and pricks her legs.* JOAN *curses and screams throughout.* PACKER *and* GOODY *abuse her: a short sharp moment of great noise and confusion.*

GOODY: Hold still you old witch. Devil not help you now, no good calling him. Strong for your age, that's the devil's strength in her, see. Hold still, you stinking old strumpet . . .

PACKER: Hold your noise, witch, how can we tell what we're doing? Ah, ah, there's for you devil, there's blood, and there's blood, where's your spot, we'll find you out Satan . . .

JOAN: Damn you to hell, oh Christ help me! Ah, ah, you're hurting, let go, damn you, oh sweet God, oh you devils, oh devil take you . . .

PACKER: There, there, no blood here, Goody Haskins. Here's her spot. Hardly a speck here.

GOODY: How she cries the old liar, pretending it hurts her.

PACKER: There's one for hanging, stand aside there. We've others to attend to. Next please, Goody.

GOODY *takes* ALICE. PACKER *helps, and her skirts are thrown over her head while he pricks her. She tries not to cry out.*

GOODY: Why so much blood?

PACKER: The devil's cunning here.

GOODY: She's not crying much, she can't feel it.

PACKER: Have I the spot though? Which is the spot? There. There. There. No, I haven't the spot. Oh, it's tiring work. Set this one aside. Maybe there's others will speak against her and let us know more clearly what she is.

ALICE *is stood aside.*

PACKER: If anyone here knows anything more of this woman why she might be a witch, I charge them in God's name to speak out, or the guilt of filthy witchcraft will be on you for concealing it.

SUSAN: I know something of her.

PACKER: Don't be shy then girl, speak out.

ALICE: Susan, what you doing? Don't speak against me.

SUSAN: Don't let her at me.

ALICE: You'll have me hanged.

SUSAN *starts to shriek hysterically.*

GOODY: Look, she's bewitched.

MARGERY: It's Alice did it to her.

ALICE: Susan, stop.

SUSAN: Alice. Alice. Alice.

PACKER: Take the witch out and the girl may be quiet.

GOODY *takes* ALICE *off.* SUSAN *stops.*

MARGERY: See that.

JACK: Praise God I escaped such danger.

SUSAN: She met with the devil, she told me, like a man in black she met him in the night and did uncleanness with him, and ever after she was not herself but wanted to be with the devil again. She took me to a cunning woman and they made me take a foul potion to destroy the baby in my womb and it was destroyed. And the cunning woman said she would teach Alice her wicked magic, and she'd have powers and not everyone could learn that, but Alice could because she's a witch, and the cunning woman gave her something to call the devil, and she tried to call him, and she made a puppet, and stuck pins in, and tried to make me believe that was the devil, but that was my baby girl, and next day she was sick and her face blue and limbs all twisted up and she died. And I don't want to see her.

PACKER: These cunning women are worst of all. Everyone hates witches who do harm but good witches they go to for help and come into the devil's power without knowing it. The infection will spread through the whole country if we don't stop it. Yes, all witches deserve death, and the good witch even more than the bad one. Oh God, do not let your kingdom be overrun by the devil. And you, girl, you went to this good witch, and you destroyed the child in your womb by witchcraft, which is a grievous offence. And you were there when this puppet was stuck with pins, and consented to the death of your own baby daughter?

SUSAN: No, I didn't. I didn't consent. I never wished her harm. Oh if I was angry sometimes or cursed her for crying, I never meant it. I'd take it back if I could have her back. I never meant to harm her.

PACKER: You can't take your curses back, you cursed her to death. That's two of your children you killed. And what other harm have you done? Don't look amazed, you'll speak soon enough. We'll prick you as you pricked your babies.

Scene Fifteen

GOODY *takes* SUSAN *and* PACKER *pulls up her skirt.*

GOODY: There's no man finds more witches than Henry Packer. He can tell by their look, he says, but of course he has more ways that that. He's read all the books and he's travelled. He says the

reason there's so much witchcraft in England is England is too soft with its witches, for in Europe and Scotland they are hanged and burned and if they are not penitent they are burnt alive, but in England they are only hanged. And the ways of discovering witches are not so good here, for in other countries they have thumbscrews and racks and the bootikens which is said to be the worst pain in the world, for it fits tight over the legs from ankle to knee and is driven tighter and tighter till the legs are crushed as small as might be and the blood and marrow spout out and the bones crushed and the legs made unserviceable forever. And very few continue their lies and denials then. In England we haven't got such thorough ways, our ways are slower but they get the truth in the end when a fine skilful man like Henry Packer is onto them. He's well worth the twenty shillings a time, and I get the same, which is very good of him to insist on and well worth it though some folk complain and say, 'what, the price of a cow, just to have a witch hanged?' But I say to them think of the expense a witch is to you in the damage she does to property, such as a cow killed one or two pounds, a horse maybe four pounds, besides all the pigs and sheep at a few shillings a time, and chickens at sixpence all adds up. For two pounds and our expenses at the inn, you have all that saving, besides knowing you're free of the threat of sudden illness and death. Yes, it's interesting work being a searcher and nice to do good at the same time as earning a living. Better than staying home a widow. I'd end up like the old women you see, soft in the head and full of spite with their muttering and spells. I keep healthy keeping the country healthy. It's an honour to work with a great professional.

Scene Sixteen

BETTY: I'm frightened to come any more. They'll say I'm a witch.

ELLEN: Are they saying I'm a witch?

BETTY: They say because I screamed that was the devil in me. And when I ran out of the house they say where was I going if not to meet other witches. And some know I come to see you.

ELLEN: Nobody's said it yet to my face.

BETTY: But the doctor says he'll save me. He says I'm not a witch, he says I'm ill. He says I'm his patient so I can't be a witch. He says he's making me better. I hope I can be better.

ELLEN: You get married, Betty, that's safest.

BETTY: But I want to be left alone. You know I do.

ELLEN: Left alone for what? To be like me? There's no doctor going to save me from being called a witch. Your best chance of being left alone is marry a rich man, because it's part of his honour to have a wife who does nothing. He has his big house and rose garden and trout stream, he just needs a fine lady to make it complete and you can be that. You can sing and sit on the lawn and change your dresses and order the dinner. That's the best you can do. What would you rather? Marry a poor man and work all day? Or go on as you're going, go on strange? That's not safe. Plenty of girls feel like you've been feeling, just for a bit. But you're not one to go on with it.

BETTY: If it's true there's witches, maybe I've been bewitched. If the witches are stopped, maybe I'll get well.

ELLEN: You'll get well, my dear, and you'll get married, and you'll tell your children about the witches.

BETTY: What's going to happen? Will you be all right?

ELLEN: You go home now. You don't want them finding you here.

BETTY *goes.*

I could ask to be swum. They think the water won't keep a witch in, for Christ's baptism sake, so if a woman floats she's a witch. And if she sinks they have to let her go. I could sink. Any fool can sink. It's how to sink without drowning. It's whether they get you out. No, why should I ask to be half drowned? I've done nothing. I'll explain to them what I do. It's healing, not harm. There's no devil in it. If I keep calm and explain it, they can't hurt me.

If You Float

If you float you're a witch
If you scream you're a witch
If you sink, then you're dead anyway.
If you cure you're a witch
Or impure you're a witch
Whatever you do, you must pay.
Fingers are pointed, a knock at the door,
You may be a mother, a child or a whore.
If you complain you're a witch
Or you're lame you're a witch
Any marks or deviations count for more.
Got big tits you're a witch
Fall to bits you're a witch
He likes them young, concupiscent and
                                            poor.
Fingers are pointed, a knock at the door,
They're coming to get you, do you know
                                         what for?
So don't drop a stitch
My poor little bitch
If you're making a spell
Do it well.
Deny it you're bad
Admit it you're mad
Say nothing at all
They'll damn you to hell.

Scene Seventeen

ALICE *is tied up, sitting on the floor.*
GOODY *is eating and yawning.*

GOODY: You'd better confess, my dear, for he'll have you watched night and day and there's nothing makes a body so wretched as not sleeping. I'm tired myself. It's for your own good, you know, to save you from the devil. If we let you stay as you are, you'd be damned eternally and better a little pain now than eternal . . . (*She realizes* ALICE *is nodding to sleep and picks up a drum and bangs it loudly. She gives it several bangs to keep* ALICE *awake.* PACKER *comes in.*) She's an obstinate young witch, this one, on her second night. She tires a body out.

PACKER: Go and sleep, Goody, I'll watch her a while.

GOODY: You're a considerate man, Mr Packer. We earn our money.

GOODY *goes.*

PACKER: I'm not a hard man. I like to have my confession so I'm easy in my mind I've done right.

ALICE: Where's my boy?

PACKER: Safe with good people.

ALICE: He wants me.

PACKER: He's safe from the devil, where you'll never come.

ALICE: I want him.

PACKER: Why won't you confess and make this shorter?

ALICE: It isn't true.

PACKER: Tell me your familiars. Tell me your imps' names. I won't let them plague you for telling. God will protect you if you repent.

ALICE: I haven't any. (PACKER *drums.*) I want my boy.

PACKER: Then you should have stayed home at night with him and not gone out after the devil.

ALICE: I want him.

PACKER: How could a mother be a filthy witch and put her child in danger?

ALICE: I didn't.

PACKER: Night after night, it's well known.

ALICE: But what's going to happen to him? He's only got me.

PACKER: He should have a father. Who's his father? Speak up, who's his father?

ALICE: I don't know.

PACKER: You must speak.

ALICE: I don't know.

PACKER: You must confess.

PACKER *drums.*

ALICE: Oh my head. Please don't. Everything's drumming.

PACKER: I'll watch. Your imps will come to see you.

ALICE: Drumming.

PACKER *suddenly stops.*

PACKER: Ah. Ah. What's this? A spider. A huge black one. And it ran off when it saw a godly man. Deny if you can that spider's one of your imps.

ALICE: No.

PACKER: Then why should it come? Tell me that.

ALICE: I want my boy.

PACKER: Why? Why do you keep on about the boy? Who's his father? Is the devil his father?

ALICE: No, no, no.

PACKER: I'll have the boy to see me in the morning. If he's not the devil's child he'll speak against you. (ALICE *cries.*) I'll watch you. I've watched plenty of witches and hanged them all. I'll get that spider too if it comes back.

Scene Eighteen

GOODY *is shaving* SUSAN *under the arm.*

GOODY: There, that's the second arm done, and no mark yet. Devil hides his marks all kinds of places. The more secret the better he likes it. Though I knew one witch had a great pink mark on her shoulder and neck so everyone could see. And a woman last week with a big lump in her breast like another whole teat where she sucked her imps, a little black one she had and a little white one and kept them in wool in a bottle. And when I squeezed it first white stuff came out like milk and then blood, for she fed those horrid creatures on milk and blood and they sucked her secret parts in the night too. Now let's see your secret parts and see what the devil does there.

She makes SUSAN *lie down, and pulls up her skirt to shave her.* PACKER *comes in.*

PACKER: What devil's marks?

GOODY: No need to shave the other for she has three bigs in her privates almost an inch long like great teats where the devil sucks her and a bloody place on her side where she can't deny she cut a lump off herself so I wouldn't find it.

PACKER: Such a stinking old witch I won't look myself. Is there nothing here?

GOODY: She's clean yet but we'll shave her and see what shameful thing's hidden.

PACKER: Though a mark is a sure sign of a

witch's guilt having no mark is no sign of innocence for the devil can take marks off.

JOAN: And the devil take you.

PACKER: You'll be with the devil soon enough.

JOAN: And I'll be glad to see him. I been a witch these ten years. Boys was always calling after me and one day I said to a boy, 'Boy boy you call me witch but when did I make your arse to itch.' And he ran off and I met a little grey kitling and the kitling said, 'You must go with me' and I said, 'Avoid Satan.' And he said, 'You must give me your body and soul and you'll have all happiness.' And I did. And I gave him my blood every day, and that's my old cat Vinegar Tom. And he lamed John Peter's son that's a cripple this day, that was ten years ago. And I had two more imps sent me crept in my bed in the night sucked my privy parts so sore they hurt me and wouldn't leave me. And I asked them to kill Mary Johnson who crossed me and she wasted after. And everyone knows Anne that had fits and would gnash her teeth and took six strong men to hold her. That was me sent those fits to her. My little imps are like moles with four feet but no tails and a black colour. And I'd send them off and they'd come back in the night and say they did what I said. Jack is lucky I didn't bewitch him to death and Margery, but she was kind to me long ago. But I killed their cows like I killed ten cows last year. And the great storm and tempest comes when I call it and strikes down trees. But now I'm in prison my powers all gone or I'd call down thunder and twist your guts.

PACKER: Is there any reason you shouldn't be hanged?

JOAN: I'm with child.

GOODY: Who'd believe that?

Scene Nineteen

JOAN *and* ELLEN *are hanged while* MARGERY *prays.*

MARGERY: Dear God, thank you for saving us. Let us live safe now. I have scrubbed the dairy out. You have shown your power in destroying the wicked, and you show it in blessing the good. You have helped me in my struggle against the witches, help me in my daily struggle. Help me work harder and our good harvests will be to your glory. Bless Miss Betty's marriage and let her live happy. Bless Jack and keep him safe from evil and let him love me and give us the land, amen.

Scene Twenty

JOAN *and* ELLEN *hanging.*

SUSAN: Alice, how can you look? Your poor mother. You're not even crying.

ALICE: She wasn't a witch. She wouldn't know how.

SUSAN: Alice, she was.

ALICE: The cunning woman was, I think. That's why I was frightened of her.

SUSAN: I was a witch and never knew it. I killed my babies. I never meant it. I didn't know I was so wicked. I didn't know I had that mark on me. I'm so wicked. Alice, let's pray to God we won't be damned. If we're hanged, we're saved, Alice, so we mustn't be frightened. It's done to help us. Oh God, I know now I'm loathsome and a sinner and Mr Packer has shown me how bad I am and I repent I never knew that but now I know and please forgive me and don't make me go to hell and be burnt forever –

ALICE: I'm not a witch.

SUSAN: Alice, you know you are. God, don't hear her say that.

ALICE: I'm not a witch. But I wish I was. If I could live I'd be a witch now after what they've done. I'd make wax men and melt them on a slow fire. I'd kill their animals and blast their crops and make such storms, I'd wreck their ships all over the world. I shouldn't have been frightened of Ellen, I should have learnt. Oh if I could meet with the devil now I'd give him anything if he'd give me power. There's no way for us except by the devil. If I only did have magic, I'd make them feel it.

Lament for the Witches

Where have the witches gone?

Who are the witches now?
Here we are.

All the gentle witches' spells
blast the doctors' sleeping pills.
The witches hanging in the sky
haunt the courts where lawyers lie.
Here we are.

They were gentle witches
with healing spells.
They were desperate witches
with no way out but the other side of hell.

A witch's crying in the night
switches out your children's light.
All your houses safe and warm
are struck at by the witches' storm.
Here we are.

Where have all the witches gone?
Who are the witches now?
Here we are.

They were gentle witches
with healing spells.
They were desperate witches
with no way out but the other side of hell.
Here we are.

Look in the mirror tonight.
Would they have hanged you then?
Ask how they're stopping you now.
Where have the witches gone?
Who are the witches now?
Ask how they're stopping you now.
Here we are.

Scene Twenty-One

SPRENGER: He's Kramer.

KRAMER: He's Sprenger.

KRAMER:
SPRENGER: Professors of Theology

KRAMER: delegated by letters apostolic

SPRENGER: (here's a toast, non-alcoholic).

KRAMER: Inquisitors of heretical pravities

SPRENGER: we must fill those moral cavities

KRAMER: so we've written a book

SPRENGER: *Malleus Maleficarum*

KRAMER: *The Hammer of Witches.*

SPRENGER: It works like a charm

KRAMER: to discover witches

SPRENGER: and torture with no hitches.

KRAMER: Why is a greater number of witches found in the fragile feminine sex than in men?

SPRENGER: Why is a greater number of witches found in the fragile feminine sex than in men?

KRAMER: 'All wickedness is but little to the wickedness of a woman.' Ecclesiastes.

SPRENGER: Here are three reasons, first because

KRAMER: woman is more credulous and since the aim of the devil is to corrupt faith he attacks them. Second because

SPRENGER: women are more impressionable. Third because

KRAMER: women have slippery tongues and cannot conceal from other women what by their evil art they know.

SPRENGER: Women are feebler in both body and mind so it's not surprising.

KRAMER: In intellect they seem to be of a different nature from men –

SPRENGER: like children.

KRAMER: Yes.

SPRENGER: But the main reason is

KRAMER: she is more carnal than
SPRENGER: a man

KRAMER: as may be seen from her many carnal abominations.

SPRENGER: She was formed from a bent rib

KRAMER: and so is an imperfect animal.

SPRENGER: Fe mina, female, that is fe faith minus without

KRAMER: so cannot keep faith.

SPRENGER: A defect of intelligence.

KRAMER: A defect of inordinate passions.

SPRENGER: They brood on vengeance.

KRAMER: Wherefore it is no wonder
SPRENGER: they are witches.

KRAMER: Women have weak memories.

SPRENGER: Follow their own impulses.

KRAMER: Nearly all the kingdoms of the world have been overthrown by women

SPRENGER: as Troy, etc.

KRAMER: She's a liar by nature

SPRENGER: vain

KRAMER: more bitter than death

SPRENGER: contaminating to touch

KRAMER: their carnal desires

SPRENGER: their insatiable malice

KRAMER: their hands are as bands for binding when they place their hands on a creature to bewitch it with the help of the devil.

SPRENGER: To conclude.

KRAMER: All witchcraft

SPRENGER: comes from carnal lust

KRAMER: which is in woman

KRAMER:
SPRENGER: insatiable.

KRAMER: It is no wonder there are more women than men found infected with the heresy of witchcraft.

SPRENGER: And blessed be the Most High, which has so far preserved the male sex from so great a crime.

Evil Women

Evil women
Is that what you want?
Is that what you want to see?
On the movie screen
Of your own wet dream
Evil women.

If you like sex sinful, what you want is us.
You can be sucked off by a succubus.
We had this man, and afterwards he died.

Does she do what she's told or does she nag?
Are you cornered in the kitchen by a
                                    bitching hag?
Satan's lady, Satan's pride.
Satan's baby, Satan's bride,
A devil woman's not easily satisfied.

Do you ever get afraid
You don't do it right?
Does your lady demand it
Three times a night?
If we don't say you're big

Do you start to shrink?
We earn our own money
And buy our own drink.

Did you learn you were dirty boys, did you
                                        learn
Women were wicked to make you burn?
Satan's lady, Satan's pride,
Satan's baby, Satan's bride,
Witches were wicked and had to burn.

Evil women
Is that what you want?
Is that what you want to see?
In your movie dream
Do they scream and scream?
Evil women
Evil women
Women.

Vinegar Tom

I first met Monstrous Regiment on a march, abortion I think, early in 1976. I ran into Chris Bowler and she introduced me to some of the others. Chris said the company were thinking they would like to do a play about witches; so was I, though it's hard now to remember what ideas I was starting from. I think I had already read *Witches, Midwives and Nurses* by Barbara Ehrenreich and Deirdre English. Certainly it had a strong influence on the play I finally wrote.

Soon I met the whole company to talk about working with them. They gave me a list of books they had read and invited me to a rehearsal of *Scum*. I left the meeting exhilarated. I'd been writing plays for eighteen years, half my life: for the stage as a student, then a lot of radio, then in 1972 *Owners*, followed by *Moving Clocks Go Slow*, *Objections to Sex and Violence*, all done at the Royal Court; a few weeks earlier I had finished *Traps*. All this work had been completely solitary – I never discussed my ideas while I was writing or showed anyone anything earlier than a final polished draft. So this was a new way of working, which was one of its attractions. Also a touring company, with a wider audience; also a feminist company – I felt briefly shy and daunted, wondering if I would be acceptable, then immensely happy and stimulated by the discovery of shared ideas and the enormous energy and feeling of possibilities in the still new company.

I was about to do a play for Joint Stock, who excited me for some of the same reasons, some different. There wasn't a lot of time, and the two plays, *Vinegar Tom* and *Light Shining in Buckinghamshire*, overlapped both in time and ideas. All I knew at this point about the Joint Stock project was that it was going to be about the English Revolution in the 1640s, what people had wanted from it, and particularly the millenial expectations of the Ranters. A lot of what I was learning about the period, religion, class, the position of women, was relevant to both plays.

Over Easter on Dartmoor I read books, Monstrous Regiment's suggestions and others I had found; rapidly left aside the interesting theory that witchcraft had existed as a survival of suppressed pre-Christian religions and went instead for the theory that witchcraft existed in the minds of its persecutors, that 'witches' were a scapegoat in times of stress like Jews and blacks. I discovered for the first time the extent of Christian teaching against women and saw the connections between medieval attitudes to witches and continuing attitudes to women in general. The women accused of witchcraft were often those on the edges of society, old, poor, single, sexually unconventional; the old herbal medical tradition of the cunning woman was suppressed by the rising professionalism of the male doctor. I didn't base the play on any precise historical events, but set it rather loosely in the seventeenth century, partly because it was the time of the last major English witchhunts, and partly because the social upheavals, class changes, rising professionalism and great hardship among the poor were the context of the kind of witchhunt I wanted to write about; partly of course because it was the period I was already reading about for Joint Stock. One of the things that struck me reading the detailed accounts of witch trials in Essex (*Witchcraft in Tudor and Stuart England*, Macfarlane) was how petty and everyday the witches' offences were, and how different the atmosphere of actual English witchhunts seemed to be from my received idea, based on slight knowledge of the European witchhunts and films and fiction, of burnings, hysteria and sexual orgies. I wanted to write a play about witches with no witches in it; a play not about evil, hysteria and possession by the devil but about poverty, humiliation and prejudice, and how the women accused of witchcraft saw themselves.

I met Monstrous Regiment again, talked over the ideas I had so far, and found the same aspects of witchcraft appealed to them too. Then I went off and wrote a first draft of the play, very quickly, in about three days. I may have written one or two songs at this stage but not all of them. The company were happy to accept this first draft and leave rewriting till after my work with Joint Stock, which was lucky as in May I started the Joint Stock workshop. June-July I wrote *Light Shining*, rehearsed through August, and it opened at the Edinburgh festival. Then I met Monstrous Regiment again. Helen Glavin had been working on the music for the songs during the summer. I worked on the text again, expanding it slightly. It was only at this stage that Josefina Cupido joined the company and I wrote in the character of Betty, who didn't exist before and who filled a need that had come up in discussion for a character under pressure to make a conventional marriage. 'Why am I tied' was originally from a scene that never fitted in *Light Shining*, part of Hoskins' early life! During rehearsals I remember Gillian Hanna who played Alice, pointing out that Alice's child was mentioned early in the play but not after she was in prison, and I sat at a table in the corner of the rehearsal room and wrote the scene where Packer asks if it is the devil's child. It was a very easy and enjoyable co-operation with the company. My habit of solitary working and shyness at showing what I wrote at an early stage had been wiped out by the even greater self-exposure in Joint Stock's method of work. And our shared view of what the play was about and our commitment to it made rewriting precise and easy. I particularly enjoyed working on the songs with Helen Glavin, and again this was something I hadn't done before – but did again the next year, working on Monstrous Regiment's cabaret *Floorshow* with Michelene Wandor and Bryony Lavery. By the time *Traps* was done at the Theatre Upstairs in January 1977 it seemed more than a year since I had written it. Though I still wanted to write alone sometimes, my attitude to myself, my work and others had been basically and permanently changed by the two shows I had written since, for Joint Stock and Monstrous Regiment.

Production Note

When *Vinegar Tom* was originally published by Theatre Quarterly I included almost no stage directions. I always prefer to keep them to a minimum and as I was with the company throughout rehearsal there was no need to write anything down. A couple of productions since then, in San Francisco and at Smith College, Mass., made me realise that I should have pointed out that the songs, which are contemporary, should if possible be sung by actors in modern dress. They are not part of the action and not sung by the characters in the scenes before them. In the original company all the actors could sing so it was no problem for some members of the company to be out of costume at any time to be in the band. Obviously this may not always be possible. But it is essential that the actors are not in character when they sing the songs.

Another point is that the pricking scene is one of humiliation rather than torture and that Packer is an efficient professional, not a sadistic maniac.

It's important that Kramer and Sprenger are played by women. Originally they were played by Chris Bowler and Mary McCusker, who as Ellen and Joan had just been hanged, which seems to be an ideal doubling. They played them as Edwardian music hall gents in top hats and tails, and some of the opening rhymes and jokes are theirs. The rest of the scene is genuine Kramer and Sprenger, from their handbook on witches and women, *Malleus Maleficarum, the Hammer of Witches*.

Caryl Churchill

Vinegar Tom was Monstrous Regiment's second production. The idea for a play about witchcraft came out of the initial meetings we'd had the previous year. The list of subjects for shows was enormous, but witchcraft was always high on it. At first our knowledge of the subject was very patchy, some people had done a fair amount of reading, for others it was restricted to Hammer Horrors. But all agreed in dismissing the traditional image of the evil old crone/buxom young temptress with the pointed hat and deadly potions – we smelled a rat. We were just about to go into rehearsal with our first play, *Scum*, when we met up with Caryl Churchill and discovered – wonderful coincidence – that we all wanted to do the same play. We wasted no time in commissioning her.

We were delighted with the first draft. It said so much in so few words. We found it full of humour, passion, and above all good parts for women! There were no rewrites in the normal sense, no cuts, but we decided to introduce another character. We wanted to show the pressures and constraints of that very narrow seventeenth century society on a young noblewoman, Betty, materially better off, but with little more choice or power over her life than Alice or Susan.

Working with Caryl on the script, and later during rehearsals, was the company's first real experience of working closely with a woman writer. It hadn't been possible in the same way with Claire Luckham on *Scum* – she lives in Liverpool and had family commitments which restricted the amount of time she could spend with us. It was a very exciting and creative period for us. The need for all of us to speak the truth about these persecuted women, fired and united us, and there was a great feeling of joy in the shared enterprise. In putting the character of Betty into the play, for instance, the progress from ideas and feelings to sections of dialogue seemed amazingly quick and painless. First we discussed what we wanted to say with the character, and what scenes were needed for it. Then, whilst we rehearsed something else in one part of the rehearsal room, Caryl sat in a corner and wrote the extra scenes. At the end of the day, bingo, two new scenes. We thought to ourselves 'Ah, so *this* is what it's like working with a woman writer', and fondly imagined all our productions rolling out with equal ease and enjoyment.

Looking back, it's difficult to remember at what point the songs appeared. There may have been one or two lyrics in the first draft – it was certainly always our intention to include as much music as possible in the play. Since the beginning there had been a composer/singer/pianist in the company, Helen Glavin, and Josefina Cupido was just about to join us – having been lurking about on the edges of the company for some time. We all felt a frustration with the way we had seen music used so often in the theatre. We were determined that ours should be original in style, and should have an intellectual and creative life of its own – pushing the action along almost as much as the dialogue, not simply existing as a decoration or breathing space in the plot. Accordingly during rehearsals we decided, with Caryl, that the music should be performed in modern dress and provide a contemporary commentary on the action. The instruments (piano, congas and guitar) and the voices were all acoustic, so Helen was able to compose music that was in keeping with the period yet could strongly embrace twentieth century idioms.

The writer/group collaboration was so close, with Caryl attending all rehearsals, it isn't easy to pinpoint where specific ideas came from. One production element that certainly came from the company was the decision to cast the women's parts against what would normally be regarded as 'type'. We wanted to challenge those stereotypes, and in addition give ourselves the opportunity as actors to expand into parts normally forbidden to us because we were too young/old/thin/fat.

The play received a very interesting reaction. It gathered a different, perhaps more feminist/women's audience than *Scum*. Some men in particular were upset by it. With *Scum* (about the Paris commune of 1870-71) they felt included in the struggle of the women laundry workers, with this they were definitely placed outside the experience of the female characters. Some people felt accused by the songs, which in their manner of presentation –

as well as in the lyrics and music – were direct and uncompromising. It wasn't our intention to make people feel accused or blamed in a simplistic way, but neither did we want to let them off the hook, or allow them to distance themselves emotionally from the events of the play because they were distant historically. At the other end of the spectrum we were accused of being too heterosexual, some women found the male/female love-making of the first scene offensive. This was the company's first taste of critical reaction to our politics from other women, and it was very chastening. The climate of the media, and to some extent public reaction, towards feminism has changed so much during the life-time of Monstrous Regiment. It has gone from unpopular to trendy to passé, and reaction to our work has zig-zagged with it. At first (when there were very few feminist/women's groups) it often felt as though we were urgently required to embody every shade of feminist belief, and whenever we represented one person we negated another.

The reaction from reviewers on the whole was very favourable, even if they weren't keen on the politics of the play, they couldn't deny the strength of the writing. When Ned Chaillet of *The Times* described it as 'a picture slightly different from the one handed down through legend and historical records', we knew we'd succeeded.

Two last notes. The Pricking: We used stage blood only in the pricking scene with Packer and Alice, and here it was very effective – causing several people to faint or be helped retching from the theatre. The Hanging: We decided to make this as realistic as possible, using a wooden frame and climbing harnesses under Mary and Chris' nightdresses – which were hooked on to trick nooses. Nevertheless it was widely believed that they were dummies, more attention being paid to the Alice/Susan scene going on in front, and Mary and Chris are still complaining about damage to their spines.

Monstrous Regiment

Caryl Churchill

Stage plays

Owners (Royal Court 1972). Owners in property and relationships; a comedy. A woman property developer finds what she's capable of. Published Eyre Methuen, 1973.

Moving Clocks Go Slow (Royal Court 1975). Sci-fi play.

Objections to Sex and Violence (Royal Court 1975). Terrorism and seaside.

Traps (Royal Court 1977). An impossible object. Published Pluto Press, 1978.

Vinegar Tom (Monstrous Regiment 1976). Seventeenth century witchhunt; songs about women now. Published Theatre Quarterly Publications, 1978.

Light Shining in Buckinghamshire (Joint Stock 1976). How the English revolution didn't happen. Published Pluto Press, 1977.

Floorshow (Monstrous Regiment 1977). Sketches and lyrics for cabaret about women and work.

Cloud Nine (Joint Stock 1979). About sexual politics in colonial Africa and present-day England. Published Pluto Press, 1979.

Three More Sleepless Nights (Soho Poly 1980). Short play. Two couples try to change.

DUSA, FISH, STAS & VI

The original production of *Dead Fish* took place at Kundry's Theatre, Edinburgh, in August 1976 with the following cast:

VIOLET	Lindsay Ingram
STAS	Lesley Joseph
FISH	Jennie Stoller
DUSA	Sally Watts
SINGER	Barbara Jung
MUSICIANS	Bruce Douglas (bass)
	Richard Sanders (piano)
	Simon Saunders (drums)

Directed by Caroline Eves
Music and lyrics by Paul Sand
Sound by Pavel Kubes

Dusa, Fish, Stas and Vi was initially presented by the Hampstead Theatre Club, London, on 8 December 1976 and was subsequently presented by Michael Codron, by arrangement with the Hampstead Theatre Club, at the Mayfair Theatre, London, on 10 February 1977. The cast was as follows:

VIOLET	Mary Maddox
STAS	Diane Fletcher
FISH	Alison Fiske
DUSA	Brigit Forsyth

Directed by Nancy Meckler
Designed by Tanya McCallin
Costumes by Lindy Hemming
Lighting by Gerry Jenkinson

Notes on the characters

DUSA is a tall girl with an eye for line, dimension and colour, ex-Royal College. She has the slight incoherence of someone whose talent is for the spatial. Her clothes, though not new, are *dernier cri* . . . she has two small children and is not working . . . and she wears them with angular elegance. She is not overtly 'motherly', because she has two children, i.e., she is not soppy, or pea-brained or henlike. She *is* split, displaying the angst and the particular vulnerability of the breeding bitch; also the restless boredom. DUSA is pronounced Dooza.

FISH has all the natural authority and self-confidence of the upper-middle classes. She is from a background of intellectuals; there may be Huxleys, Rowntrees in her pedigree. She is passionate and caring, searching with courage for the now . . . the way . . . confrontation without spite, without predication. Having considered the inadvertency of her privilege, and the mores of middle-class values, she has attached herself to a political group on the left, and is seeking to find a supportable, adventurous and equitable way of life with her long-standing lover.

STAS is the daughter of a tenant farmer. She has been bred in the country, pulled out calves' forelegs because her arms were small enough. She works as a physiotherapist in a London hospital, and has a passion for science . . . for how. The why of life seems to her to be a meaningless question. She is a hostess at night, sleeping with men for high fees. She is discreet, efficient, reliable and gives good value. Her objective is to save enough money to go to Hawaii to study marine biology. Stas, during the day, is a large, strong woman, with a steady stare, unsmiling. Her metamorphosis from physiotherapist to hostess is startling. Before our eyes she transforms herself from an unremarkable female employee to a glittering, heavy-headed, mesmeric-eyed Klimt painting. Her clothes, for her evening work, are expensive, well-cut and discreetly attractive. They are not in the least whorish. STAS is pronounced Stass.

VIOLET is younger than the others. A waif probably given house room by Fish. Violet is anorexic. At the beginning of the play she is physically weak, and not well. After a brief stay in hospital she is on uppers and perked up. She is one of the vast numbers of working-class adolescents who are bright, restless or maladjusted enough to leave home and hit London, or any capital city.

Act One

*A space, not naturalistic. Neutral in atmos-
phere. One or two pieces of 'good' furniture.
There is a divan and a large, very fine,
double-doored French armoire.*

*A small black and white television is switched
on, but without sound.*

DUSA *enters. She is in her late twenties.
Tall, leggy, with battered but very fashion-
able clothes, stylishly worn. We could take
her for a Vogue fashion model off-duty. She
has a weekend-sized shoulder bag. She looks
round, sees no one, crosses, switches off the
television.*

VI: You're in the way. What are you doing!

DUSA *jumps. We now see VI, who sits
up. She has been lying on the floor in her
overcoat, with the rug pulled over her,
watching the television.*

DUSA: Oh, sorry . . . are you watching?
What's the matter, is the heating off?

VI: I'm cold.

DUSA: It's boiling in here! Where's Fish?

VI *shrugs without answering. DUSA
looks at her and goes out.*

DUSA (*off*): Fish . . . Fish?

She returns, stands over VI.

VI: They're in Bridport.

DUSA: Who? Who? (*She crosses, switches
off the television, turns on VI. We realise
that she is angry.*)

VI: They got married.

DUSA (*puzzled*): Married? (*Realisation
dawns.*) They got married! You're joking
– you mean Alan?

VI: Nah . . . Robert Redford. (*She hunches
the rug up around herself.*)

DUSA: But why didn't she tell me?! We
were supposed to meet. (*She moves away,
angry.*)

VI (*flicker of interest for the first time*): Did
you get it?

DUSA: What? Oh . . . yeah. Look, when
did they decide –

VI: Friday.

DUSA: Why didn't she tell me? I could
have got someone else . . . I was stuck
there *hours* with this pissy little lawyer.

*She switches on the radio, starts to undo
her bag, takes out a deep purple kimono.
VI gets up, crosses, approaches, touches
the kimono.*

VI: This yours?

DUSA: Have it. Have it!

*VI drops the rug, puts the kimono on over
her coat and switches on the television
again.*

STAS *enters. A tallish, plain, competent-
looking girl in a white overall under her
dowdy coat. She hangs up her coat, opens
the armoire which, opened, is like
Aladdin's cave. It is lined with silver and
brimming with clothes, shimmering,
sparkling, with shelves dripping jewellery
and scarves. Above all there are at least
four fine fur coats. She strips, finds a
shower cap, throws on a towelling wrap,
grabs a handful of underwear and goes, all
with speed and precision.*

DUSA (*without interest*): Who's that?

VI: Stas.

DUSA: What?

VI: Stas . . . Stas! Turn it down!

DUSA: What?

VI: . . . the noise! I can't stand the noise!

*She glares, then returns to her corner,
which is stacked with her belongings.
DUSA, startled by VI's shriek, takes all
this in. She turns off the radio.*

DUSA: Are you living here now?

VI: Yeah, why . . . you coming back?

DUSA: With two kids?

VI(*alarmed*): Where are they?

DUSA: On the doorstep – wanna babysit
. . . they're with my mother! Tea?

*VI shakes her head. DUSA goes out,
bumping into STAS who enters, drying
herself. Her underwear is now glamorous,
pale camiknickers with expensive lace.
She zips herself into a discreet black dress
and makes up swiftly, putting up her hair,
transforming herself before our eyes into a
creature of sumptuous and startling
beauty. She drops a lipstick. DUSA,*

returning with a mug of tea, picks it up and gives it to her. She takes it without turning her head.

STAS: Thanks.

VI: How's Jagger?

STAS: Coming on. I got some good eye movements today, he was definitely following. (*She pauses, selects a fur coat, puts it over her shoulders.*) See you. (*She goes.*)

DUSA: What did you say her name was?

VI: Stas. Short for Anastasia . . . she's got a daft mother. She's working with this kid. (*She sticks out her lower lip, making a hideous face, and speaks in a mutilated way:*) . . . brain damaged. Ugh! (*As DUSA offers her a bag of cakes.*)

DUSA: I take it you're still not eating. (*She stands, wolfing a cake and drinking needily. Chewing:*) Are they all hers . . . the coats? (*She crosses, fondles them.*) Fantastic . . . she got a rich father or something?

VI(*moody*): I wouldn't be seen dead in them.

DUSA (*scoffs*): Hah!

VI: Listen . . . every fur coat is a stolen coat.

DUSA (*agreeing*): Oh I know.

But VI cuts across, suddenly slapping herself and rocking with private laughter, hinnying like a donkey.

DUSA (*suffers it for a bit, then*): Have you seen a doctor lately?

VI: Not since me last abortion. I was seven months, it was ever so strong . . . you could hear it crying all the way to the incinerator.

DUSA (*murderous*): Shuddup!

She takes out a small picture of her children, sets it by the divan.

VI (*alarmed*): How long you stopping?

DUSA: Look, don't you *ever* go out?

VI: Nope.

DUSA: Why not!

VI: What for?

DUSA stands, sits, stands again, picks up the cup. It is empty, puts it down. She has come to the end of herself, doesn't know

whether to stand, sit or scream, sits as the panic begins to rise.

DUSA: Oh God.

FISH appears in her doorway, glowing and vital. She wears government surplus clothes, carries a small rucksack.

FISH (*warm surprise*): Hu-llo! Christ. I forgot.

DUSA rises at the sight of FISH, breaks down. She lowers her head, trying to contain herself.

FISH: Oh my love, I'm so sorry! (*She embraces DUSA.*) How could I? I forgot!

DUSA (*muffled*): It doesn't matter.

FISH: What could I have been think –

DUSA: No, I'm sorry –

FISH: No, no . . . listen, did you get it?

DUSA *nods.*

FISH: What about a drink, have a drink . . .

She gestures urgently to VI, who does nothing, so FISH rushes about, slopping drink into glasses.

DUSA: Look, honestly, it doesn't matter, it was all right, really. (*She drinks, coughing and sniffing, trying to smile.*) Honestly.

FISH: Bastard. Here. (*She tops up DUSA's glass.*) You'll be all right.

DUSA: Sure. I did everything for that bugger, you know. Worked all through the pregnancies, I even washed his bloody socks!

VI(*sepulchral*): Christ.

DUSA (*after another generous swig*): When I met that guy . . . when I met that guy . . . he wore vests! (*Slight pause.*)

FISH (*consoling*): I know.

DUSA: And he had spots. All over his face . . . and all over his bum.

FISH: I know.

VI: How . . . how d'you know?

FISH: Shuddup.

DUSA: You should have seen his record collection . . . Swingles . . . Abba – once, when he thought I was out, he was listening to Andy Williams. And joining in.

They shake their heads.

DUSA: As for the gear . . . where could you take him . . . I mean – you saw!

FISH: Oh I don't know . . . last time we met he looked quite ethnic, didn't he, Vi?

DUSA: See what I mean! I even did the bloody wall stippling so's he could sit in the lav reading his Chomsky. It's so unfair. Nobody could have worshipped his cock more than I did. I ask myself . . . where does it all get you? Where?

She happens to catch VI's eye on the last.

VI (*aggressive*): What?

DUSA: Oh fuck off. I mean to say . . . what about the kids?

FISH: You'll manage.

DUSA (*bleak*): How?

FISH: Just got to be tough, that's all.

DUSA: No. No, that's just the trouble. You can't. Not with kids . . . not when you're with children. Look, you have to be gentle . . . you're bigger than they are! Remember when you were small, how big and loud and ugly grownups were. You have to get off . . . go with it . . . why not? I like all that . . . Christmas trees, making things . . . you do it for love. Why not?

Silence.

I don't want to be tough.

FISH *shrugs.*

Look, you don't know what it's like. You haven't been there. It changes you. There has to be something you do for love.

FISH: Has he assigned the lease?

DUSA: Fish, he can't afford two places . . . the house is in his name, he'll sell it. I still can't take it in, you know, I'm still shocked . . . I mean . . . overnight . . . as if I were a stranger. One day it was forever – kids, dog, goldfish . . . all of a sudden – off! One day he's their father . . . something just walks across his path . . . bingo! What have I chosen for them . . . it never occurred to me – I trusted the bugger! (*Violently, to* VI, *who is looming.*) Oh, stop it!!

VI: What's the matter with you?

FISH(*pushing* VI *aside*): You're going to have to start fighting.

DUSA: I'm not the type. Haven't the energy for a start. Look, somebody has to take time off and have the kids – she chucks hers in the fire.

FISH: Sure.

DUSA: I chose it! I knew what I was doing. . .

FISH: Sure.

DUSA: Why should I have to apologise! I lifted up my tits and went into a beautiful dream . . . and why not? Seems to me if you're not gay, or battered or one-parent you haven't got it together –

FISH: Just don't be naive, that's all.

DUSA: I wanted to be married.

FISH: OK. Great. So long as you know that you can end up skint, abandoned and hooked on valium.

DUSA: Is valium habit forming?

FISH: Depression is.

FISH *turns away.*

DUSA: I know. I know. It's just that . . . well, obviously today I'm a bit . . . you know, being in court and seeing him and everything.

FISH: He was there?

DUSA (*with difficulty*): Yup.

FISH: And I fucking forgot about it.

DUSA (*remembers*): You got married!

FISH: Oh, Vi told you.

DUSA: I couldn't believe it! Whose idea was it, yours or Alan's?

FISH (*cutting across*): Alan? It wasn't Alan, did she say it was Alan . . . oh, for Christ's sakes, Vi – she'll say anything.

DUSA: Who is it then?

FISH: Oh, some gink.

DUSA: What's his name?

FISH: Dunno . . . anyway, I've left him.

VI
DUSA } (*together*): What?

VI: What for?

FISH: I don't know. There didn't seem to be much point. Perhaps it was the weather.

Slight pause.

DUSA: What were you doing in Bridport?

FISH: His brother lives there.

DUSA: Oh.

FISH: It's not important. We stayed on this farm.

DUSA: What went wrong?

FISH: Hard to say. We kept bumping into each other and apologising. And then, this morning – I boiled a piece of ham last night, his brother's wife's in hospital. Anyway, they were sitting round expectantly so I said I'd get some breakfast. I don't know . . . I picked up the carving knife . . . he was sitting at the table on one of those mod stools . . . you know, tipping backwards and forwards. I went to cross behind him and I had this terrible feeling I wanted to stick it in his back . . . that it was the correct thing to do. (*She makes a violent gesture, as with a knife.*) Gave me quite a turn.

DUSA: What did you do?

FISH: Went upstairs, sat on the bed for a bit, then chucked my stuff out the window. Nearly ruined meself on a dahlia stake.

DUSA: So he doesn't know?

FISH: Oh I should think he does by now. Took me ages to get a lift.

VI: Well, well, well. Surprise, surprise.

FISH: Oh, you're right, I should never have done it. It was only to spite Alan.

DUSA: Yes . . . what *about* Alan?

FISH: Oh, didn't I tell you? He's got another lady.

She switches on the radio, or puts on a cassette. Music up for seven beats. DUSA switches it off.

DUSA: So you haven't seen him?

FISH: Nope.

DUSA: What's she like, have you seen her?

FISH: They were in the pub together.

The telephone rings. FISH answers it, speaks quietly, puts down the telephone.

FISH: They want me to speak at some conference.

DUSA: I must ring home. What's she like?

FISH: Spindly. Poor bitch.

DUSA: What do you mean!

FISH: He saw me as I came in the bar, so he leaned over and gave her a kiss on the nose.

DUSA: Why didn't you tell me?

FISH: You had enough on your plate.

DUSA: I must ring home. Why, after all this time?

FISH: It's the politics. I don't think he can take it.

DUSA: What do you mean, it was because of him you –

FISH: Oh, OK while I was learning . . . sticking stamps on. I'm a better speaker than he is. He's a good organiser, but I'm a better speaker. All of a sudden he wants a house and garden. We should have had a child! (*She walks, restless.*) I should have done it last autumn, we both wanted it then. (*She turns to DUSA.*) It's funny, the idea of birth is suddenly very exciting. What's it like?

DUSA: I wish I were a cat or a horse. I'd have one a year. Your body wants to go on. Once it's got the hang of it.

FISH: I see. What do you do about that?

DUSA: Dunno, haven't worked it out yet. Of course you have to pretend it's all a drag. Well, hardly the fashion, is it? Kids. Plays hell with your tits.

FISH: I should have done it. The only reason I didn't is because he wanted it to shut me up.

DUSA: Oh, it does that all right.

They break apart.

Fade to black. Low light.

Music interlude.

STAS *enters. She is wearing different clothes, indicating a time gap. She jumps slightly as she almost falls over DUSA who is hunched against the divan, on the floor, hands round her knees.*

STAS: Why aren't you in bed?

DUSA: Yes . . . in a way.

STAS *nods, digesting this. She takes off her furs, shakes them regally, hangs them up.*

I knew something was up when he gave me the backgammon. He knew all about it . . . the rules.

STAS: Oh yeah?

DUSA: And one night, after we'd been screwing, he gave me a tissue to wipe myself. You smell nice.

STAS *treads over to* DUSA, *bends for* DUSA *to take a sniff.*

STAS: Tea-rose. (*She is slightly drunk.*)

DUSA: And yet he's kind! He was lovely to Eric. I knew something was wrong as soon as I saw him walking backwards.

STAS: Backwards.

DUSA: Of course, when I saw it – oh, it was terrible!

STAS: Terrible.

DUSA: His left eye, sitting on his ruff. Eric. The cat.

STAS: Ah.

DUSA: Frank was magnificent – got the vet out of bed – he was never the same, of course . . . he seemed to lose his independence, he used to follow me round all the time. It still flares up. The eye.

STAS: Go to bed.

She strides off carefully.

Light change. Music link.

VI, *on the floor, lying on her stomach, reading.*

VI (*reads aloud*): 'Not all rape is neurotic. Military rape occurs when men, emerging from battle, having killed and risked death in a sexually over-excited condition, have a profound instinct to make contact with life, in however brutal a way. The dangerous period for women is about six hours after combat. The men then subside and if the women have wisely taken to the hills they will not be assaulted on return but asked to cook, and wash socks.' (*She murmurs further, to herself, then:*) 'The Romans understood, and surrounded their arenas with brothels, to calm the frenzies of emerging spectators. Our football grounds do not have these facilities . . .' (*She mutters further, then:*) 'Men have a tendency not to disapprove of rape – that is, unless their own mother, wife, daughter or sister are involved. When this is the case they are liable to become . . .' (*She turns a page:*) '. . . hysterical.'

She claps the book shut, and staggers to her feet. She is wobbly. DUSA *enters from within, dressed for going out.*

DUSA: If you don't eat something soon you'll be dead. I'm going out, d'you want anything?

VI: No. Yeah. Get me some tincture of myrrh.

DUSA: What?

VI: Myrrh . . . myrrh . . . tincture of myrrh . . . you gone deaf?

DUSA: Myrrh? You having me on, it's in the Bible!

VI: So's milk and honey.

DUSA: Where do I get it?

VI: Chemists!

DUSA: Here, it's not anything funny is it, what's it for?

VI: Turning fellers into frogs, what d'you think?

DUSA: Can you lend me two pounds?

VI: No.

DUSA: But you've got your social security, look, I'm late for the lawyer's, I can go to the bank after.

VI: Not in my interest, cock.

DUSA: I haven't got any money, you bloody bitch!

VI: What you gonna do then?

DUSA: Bloody walk! (*She goes. The telephone rings immediately.* VI *answers.*)

VI: Yeah? Who? (*Mock regret:*) Ahh, she's just gone out. What? (*She listens, her face changing.*) Hang on, I'll get her. (*She staggers off, yells:*) Dusa!!

She seems alarmed. She crosses to the

phone.

VI: She's coming . . . she's just coming. (*She moves away . . . gestures the phone abruptly with her head as* DUSA *enters.*)

DUSA (*picks up the telephone*): Hullo . . . yes . . . yes, this is Mrs Gilpin . . . yes, there's somebody here, why? What? What? Oh no . . . no . . . oh no . . .

She looks at VI.

When did it . . . I see. Yes I see . . . no, of course I won't . . . yes, yes, that's right. No . . . well, naturally . . . yes . . . yes, I see . . . well, if you – could you – no . . . yes, all right . . . very well . . . yes, I will. (*She puts down the telephone.*)

VI: What's up?

DUSA: He's taken the children.

VI: Where?

DUSA: They don't know. He took them for a drive . . . saw my mother – didn't come back. Apparently – (*She cannot speak.*)

VI: What you gonna do?

DUSA: What the fuck can I do! I haven't got any money! How can I find the bugger when I haven't got any money! They won't even look at you, I've had all this already with the lawyers. They know the man's got it, they don't want to know, they won't even listen! (*Her voice breaks.*)

VI: How much d'you want?

DUSA: Hundreds. Lawyers . . . detectives . . . where am I going to get it!

VI *goes to* STAS's *wardrobe and brings out a shoebox. She takes out a huge roll of notes, peels some off, offers them to* DUSA.

DUSA: What is it?

VI: What do you think . . . money!

DUSA: Is it yours?

VI: It's her escort money. She's saving up to do marine biology.

DUSA: What? Escort?

VI: Hostess. (*She peels off more notes as an afterthought.*) She's going to Hawaii University. Best facilities there.

They look at the money in the shoebox.

DUSA: But where does it all come from?

VI: Where do you think? It's a hundred nicker a screw nowadays . . . more for Arabs. Where do you think she gets all that underwear – thirty quid for a pair of knickers – you a twot or something? (*She pushes the wad of notes into* DUSA's *hand.*)

DUSA: I can't take this.

VI: She won't mind. All the same if she does. Go on – steal it!

DUSA: I feel sick. (*But she clutches the money with resolve. Fervently:*) Thanks!

VI: Don't thank me.

DUSA *is confused,* VI *points her towards the door. She moves then pauses and turns. She stands, shaking with shock, quite unaware.*

DUSA: Could you come with me, please?

VI, *the agoraphobe, wavers. She loses the battle with herself, despite the emergency.*

VI (*snarls*): Are you joking? for Christ's sakes, get the bloody fuzz on him.

DUSA *goes.* VI *puts away the shoebox. She stands immobile for a pause. Then she lurches across to the television, switches on, pulls the rug over herself, and watches the picture without sound.*

FISH (*speaks directly to audience, as on a platform*): So why is Rosa Luxemburg relevant? She fought for socialism, but that was sixty years ago. Why is she important?

Well, she was a Pole, working in Germany . . . a foreigner therefore . . . a Jewess . . . short . . . crippled . . . and a woman. Not good-looking, either. Plain.

She's relevant because amongst other things she fought Lenin on the notion of the necessity for a central party of intellectuals to run a revolution. Luxemburg was not writing from comfortable exile. She took part in the German uprisings. She lost her life by it. She saw that it took the unemployed to know about being unemployed! And she believed that the mistakes made by people doing things for themselves were more valuable than any theory coming from an elitist committee.

Lenin was *for* the First World War. He saw it as an instrument of chaos, which would be followed by world revolution.

Rosa was appalled by this. She called for an immediate cessation of the war, with no recrimination, no victimisation on either side. What happened? The punitive Treaty of Versailles led directly to the German fascism of the thirties. Rosa constantly demonstrates that the emergence of women thinkers in politics modifies Marxist theory as we know it. It's not enough to be told that we may join . . . that they will let us in . . . when they need our labour force. To be outside may be oppression. To be inside may well be total irrelevancy. It's not just a matter of equal pay . . . equal opportunity. For the first time in history we have the opportunity to investigate ourselves . . . if the machines of war don't get there first. For the first time in history we are not bleeding to death . . . we are more than the receptacle for genetics. Whether our insights become realised political theory . . . a-theory . . . anti-theory, we have yet to discover. The nature of the social and political contribution of women is, at this moment, wholly in question.

Is feminism to be an increasing power elite in given existing structure? Or is that Newtonian? Who are we now? And what is to be done?

Rosa never married Leo. She never had the child she longed for. The painful hopes in the letters from prison were never to be realised. She writes to him from Zurich about seeing a fine child in a park, and wanting to scoop him up in her arms and run off with him, back to her room. Usually when people write about her nowadays they leave all that out. They are wrong.

She smiles, goes.

VI *reading.* STAS *enters, eating a lettuce sandwich.*

VI (*irritated by the sound of* STAS *eating*): Every time you bite into that lettuce it screams.

STAS: Keep it up, Skin. (*She bites, heartily, looks at the sandwich.*) Shuddup! Where's Fish?

VI: Seeing her feller.

STAS: Alan Duncan?

VI: Why, what's wrong?

STAS: It's washed up . . . why doesn't she get the message?

VI: His ears are too big. (*Pause.*)

STAS: She should give him the push. What's she trying to prove? She can slum as much as she likes, she's never going to be one of the workers.

VI: She takes it very serious.

STAS: Upper class twit, they're always the worst.

VI: Shut up.

DUSA: She should kick you out for a start.

VI: What for? What have I done?

STAS: Fallen for it.

VI: What?

STAS: The charm. Fucking Lady Bountiful. (*Sing-song:*) She's not so nice to me!

VI: Don't see why she can't do as she wants.

STAS: Forty-hour week revolutionaries . . . then it's country house time. Makes you sick.

VI: I'm not jealous of her.

STAS: Well, I am.

VI: What for?

STAS: I wanna be rich.

VI: Yeah? What about the workers?

STAS: I am the workers. (*She has been flicking through a copy of 'Nature'. Something catches her eye. She whistles.*)

VI: What?

STAS (*reading*): Nothing.

VI: What?

STAS: Read your comic.

VI: What?!

STAS (*sighs, then reads, very quickly*): 'Helium-three becomes a superfluid because of the weak attractive force between its atoms. A similar phenomenon occurs in the electrons of some other metals. However helium atoms are much larger and the dynamic tension between attraction and repulsion keeps the paired atoms at a distance. That is the unique property of the helium system.'

VI: You don't wanna believe everything you read in the papers!

STAS (*pause*): Nah, she should give him the push.

VI clears her throat dramatically as FISH enters, smiling.

Putting it all together?

FISH (*happily*): Shuddup.

VI: Did you see him?

FISH: Yup. Any tea?

VI groans but goes.

STAS: Screw?

FISH: No. We met in a caff.

STAS: What did he say?

FISH: Nothing. We just sat and drank coffee for an hour.

STAS (*non-committal*): Mmmm.

FISH: It's funny. I mean, I wasn't feeling madly in love or anything. Still . . . (*She stretches her arms, luxuriously . . .*) couldn't have been anywhere else.

STAS: So it's on?

FISH: I don't know – yes! I was just going to give him a kiss when a cat jumped on the dustbins and frightened us and then the bloody bus came. He'll ring – anyway, I shall see him down at the paper.

Music. DUSA enters from without. She is very shocked.

FISH (*waves aside VI who enters with a mug of tea*): Where are they, love?

DUSA (*shrugs*): Morocco.

VI (*proffering the tea to DUSA*): There's no extradition from Morocco.

STAS: Shut up.

FISH: What do the lawyers say?

DUSA shakes her head, unable to speak.

STAS (*gets up*): Come on, I'll run you a bath.

They go.

VI (*bursts out*): Well, it's her own fault! What did she let him treat her like dirt for? She really let herself go, it's ridiculous . . . bloody pushchairs, he got fed up with it, she looked really good when you two was together! Why don't she stand up for herself, it's ridiculous!

FISH: Don't upset yourself.

VI: I'm not.

FISH: Vi, it'll work out. Is your headache better?

VI: No!

She stumps out, ignoring the phone, which rings. FISH crosses, picks up the telephone eagerly.

FISH: Yes? Oh, Eileen, it's you . . . no, no, fine . . . when? Good . . . no, no, I can make it. Ciao. (*She puts down the telephone, makes a note in a notebook, goes.*)

Music link.

VI enters, visibly weaker. The telephone rings, but beyond looking across at it vaguely, she makes no move to answer it. The telephone stops ringing. DUSA enters, heavily tranquillised. The telephone rings again. Since it is close to VI she looks at VI. VI does not move so DUSA gets to her feet, crosses to the telephone, which stops just as she picks it up. She looks down at it, frowning in puzzlement. She puts it down, makes to pick it up again, gets muddled, and goes and sits down again.

The girls sit apart. A pause.

STAS *enters, bright and energetic. She takes a bowl of nuts from under her coat and bangs it down before VI.*

STAS: Nuts . . . !

She swoops about, opening a bottle of wine, serving the two girls, taking a wine glass from each pocket. VI does not want to eat but STAS stands over her so she takes a nut obediently. And chokes on it.

Violet . . . you are not chewing properly! (*She claps VI on the back, then refills her glass after VI has taken a drink. DUSA, meanwhile has knocked hers straight back.*)

STAS: Hey, steady on.

VI (*chewing ritualistically on a non-existent nut*): You'll fucking kill her.

STAS: Why, what's she on?

She looks on the table, then into DUSA's bag for her tablets, reads the labels.

Should be OK.

She helps herself liberally to nuts and wine, eats and drinks heartily. Pause.

I went to see that film. (*No response.*) John Wayne. (*No response.*) Mind you . . . compared to Robert Ryan, John Wayne's absolute crowshit. (*No response.*) Saw him once.

VI: Who?

STAS: In Harrods cheese department. He's a big man.

DUSA: He's dead.

Pause.

VI (*helpfully, as STAS frowns at her*): Pacino's not very big.

STAS: Neither's Hoffman. Funny really . . . Paul Newman . . . Redford . . . (*No response from DUSA.*) What about Charlie Bronson, is he small? Is Charlie Bronson small? (*No response. She turns to VI.*) Well, anyway, what have you been doing?

VI (*defensive*): Talking to her, like you said. (*She leans across to DUSA.*) What was the name of that chap?

DUSA *looks at her, uncomprehendingly.*

That chap! – oh Christ, she's bombed out of her head.

DUSA: Who?

VI: The fat one. No corsets.

DUSA: Oh, Paul Poiret.

VI: Right . . . fashion designer.

DUSA: He's dead.

VI: Look, you told me –

STAS: Oh, have a fucking nut.

VI: Haven't you got nothing else?

STAS (*diving into her coat*): Kippers!

VI: I wish you'd nick something decent.

STAS: Protein.

VI (*begins to eat one*): She can have one, I'm not eating two.

STAS (*finishing her wine and eating the rest of the nuts*): Right. What was his name?

VI: Who?

STAS: This feller . . . the fashion guy. Is he famous?

DUSA: Yes. Paul Poiret . . . Poiret . . . P-o-i-r-e-t . . .

STAS: I had got it. Any books on him?

DUSA: There's a lovely one but it's expensive.

STAS: How big is it?

DUSA: No . . . it's expensive.

STAS *goes.*

VI: Twat, she's not going to buy it. Where do you think she gets all those coats? She nicked one the other day, didn't like it, went back and got a credit. God, I feel ever so funny.

FISH *enters, her head in a newspaper.*

FISH (*to herself*): D'you know, we've fucking done it.

She stands, reading a paper, discarding it, reading the next. She becomes aware of the others.

Listen to this. 'The management conceded that the female labour force were not excessive in their demands and that there had been faults in communication.'

DUSA: What?

FISH: It means they've given in, love. (*She looks at another paper, throws it down.*) Good. Good. (*Her next speech alternates between exhaustion and spurts of energy.*)

VI: You did all right then?

FISH (*sitting*): Yeah. Good. Hah! Bloody chairman – 'I think you'll find you're speaking to the converted, ladies' – all prostate and aftershave, cunning old fucker. It was great, you should have seen us. Solid. Not a tit wobbled. God, I'm tired. (*She drinks VI's drink.*) Still. We won. All those sanctimonious union bastards trying to buy us camparis. We let them do all the shouting for the cameras.

VI (*tinge of excitement*): Are you going to be on telly?

FISH: I don't know. (*She drinks.*) I'm amazed. They're putting in a shift system to fit round school hours, and a creche.

DUSA (*frowns, apart, disapproving*): Creche?

FISH (*not hearing*): Yes, great isn't it?

DUSA (*apart*): No.

FISH: Well, it's a start. Stas is getting something to celebrate.

VI: She's drunk already.

FISH: You all right, love?

DUSA *nods.*

Alan was great . . . couldn't have been more supportive. It's awful! I mean, I feel so bad about it! He's giving her up.

VI (*belching*): What?

FISH: He's giving up his lady. (*To DUSA:*) Did you get the message about the Daily Express? (*To VI:*) Didn't you tell her? The Daily Express are coming round to take a picture of you.

DUSA: What? (*She plucks vaguely at her clothes, dimly aware of not looking good.*)

FISH: It'll help, love . . . publicity . . . get them back all the quicker. Don't worry, I won't let them bother you.

She helps herself to the last of the bottle.

It was so funny, I met her – she came over.

VI: Who?

FISH: Alan's lady.

VI: What she say?

FISH: Nothing really . . . we just stood there, the three of us, talking about the lock-out. The sun was shining . . . I mean, I liked her – I couldn't help liking her for liking him. It was stupid . . . I was so full of love I couldn't even look at him . . . I looked at his coat. God, I'm so full of it . . . (*She hugs herself joyously, with a sighing moan.*)

VI (*to DUSA*): What's up?

FISH: You OK, love?

DUSA: I don't read the Daily Express.

FISH *and* VI *laugh.*
STAS *enters. She spews shimmering gauze from her bag, followed by another exotic switch of cloth, thrown high in the air. She plonks champagne on the table, hands* DUSA *a book.*

STAS: Poiret . . . right?

FISH (*dispensing the drink and lifting her glass in a toast*): To Love . . . Freedom . . .

DUSA (*drunk*): Whhee . . .

STAS: To the moon, in June . . .

VI: What?

FISH: I'll drink to that.

VI: Don't be daft.

FISH: To the bitch goddess, success! I really think I'm ready to have a child, I've got it together in my head . . . by this time, next year, I intend to be, a mother! The kids'll be back . . . Stas'll be in Hawaii . . . and you . . . you, my girl . . . will be on a good vegetarian, compost-grown, chemical-free diet and weigh a heady seven stone!

Music.

STAS *has begun to drape* DUSA *with cloth. They all follow suit, and raid the armoire for hats, scarves and feathers. They begin to move languidly, like Poiret models. One of them opens a Japanese sunshade. Eventually* VI *climbs onto a low table and the others drape themselves about her in exaggerated poses. They freeze in an authentic tableau.*

Then DUSA, *at the front of the tableau, sags. Slowly and not without elegance she slides to the floor, flat out.*

Blackout.

Lights up on the empty stage. FISH *enters, telephones quietly for an ambulance.* STAS *enters, takes something from a drawer and goes quickly. She returns almost at once.*

FISH: I've rung for an ambulance. How is she?

STAS *shrugs, non-committal.*
DUSA *enters quietly. She is wearing the purple kimono.*

FISH: You OK?

DUSA (*nods*): The silly thing is she was eating this morning, she had some of my chocolate and half an avocado. (STAS *winces at the thought.*) She's not dying, is she?

STAS: No, of course not.

DUSA: Well, you'd know . . . she's looking a very funny colour round the mouth. (STAS *goes quickly*, DUSA *makes to follow*.)

FISH: Leave it to Stas.

DUSA: She ate nearly a whole kipper. It wasn't even cooked. I think she was trying to cheer me up. (*She shivers*.)

FISH: You feeling all right?

DUSA: Yes, I threw up the valium as well, my head's clearer.

They settle down.

Will you go and live with him again?

FISH: Yes.

DUSA: She'll move out – his other woman?

FISH: Now don't start making me feel guilty.

DUSA: I'm not.

FISH: Yes you are. She used to live with a Pole who spent her dough and socked her in the chops before gritty Alan came along with his lowland purr and swept her off her feet.

DUSA: She doesn't seem his type.

FISH: Oh, he was always a bleeding heart.

DUSA *grins at* FISH *without* FISH's *noticing*.

DUSA (*slight pause*): If I were a feller I'd be a hell of a chauvinist. All this stuff we give them about being better off. It's a load of bollocks.

FISH: What?

DUSA: They're worse off. In the old days first their mothers, then their wives . . . cradle to grave support systems.

FISH: I'm not convinced they want it. Look at Frank. Property-owning democracy? Something wrong . . . who wants to be a fucking caretaker? Got to be more to it than that.

DUSA: I think he felt left out. They were always in bed by the time he got home!

FISH: You see . . . right! Time to change the rules.

DUSA: Ho yes. And who gets left wiping the baby's bum?

FISH: We've lost the fucking group . . . worst thing we ever did . . . fucking machines . . . they'll do for us. Even kids get stuck into ghettos at five . . . well . . . what do you learn in school . . . I mean, learn! You learn by osmosis . . . by copying . . . (*The doorbell rings, she jumps up*.) That'll be the ambulance men. (*She goes*.)

DUSA *gets up, wanders about carefully, her head clearing. The telephone rings. She jumps towards it.*

DUSA: Hullo . . . no, it's Dusa. Hullo . . . how are you . . . no, not yet . . . the Embassy are going to ring me if anything – I don't know, Alan, they could have moved on, that's the worry. Do you want to speak to Fish, hang on . . . Violet's ill again, the ambulance is here . . . hang on, I'll see if I can – what? Why? (*She listens for a longish time*.) What? Oh! Oh, Alan! Oh . . . don't you think you ought to speak to her yourself . . . no, I don't . . . listen . . . hang on, will you . . . just hang on, I'll get her . . . hang on . . .

She runs out, returns, followed by FISH.

FISH: Who is it?

DUSA: Alan.

FISH: Alan? (*She picks up the phone eagerly*.) Alan . . . Alan? Hullo . . . (*She turns to* DUSA:) he must have been cut off . . . was he ringing from a phone box? What's the matter?

DUSA: They've just got married. I asked him to hang on but he said he was in a hurry.

FISH *stands still for a long time. Then, slowly, she wipes her hand into her crotch and holds it out to* DUSA *as if to indicate that she is still wet from him. She turns abruptly and goes out.*

Act Two

The same set. The telephone rings.
Eventually DUSA *enters and answers it.*

DUSA: Yes? No, she's not here.

FISH *enters. She looks unwashed and*
messy. She is smoking a cigarette.

It was for Stas.

FISH: Sure. Is she going out tonight?

DUSA: I don't know. Anyway, I'm here.

FISH: Sure. Do you know what he said? 'I
feel like a change.' I mean. And then he
said 'Don't ring me at home'. Home! I
made such a fool of myself. Crying. I
mean, I don't care . . . he's used to seeing
me in pain, when was it ever anything
else?

DUSA: Don't.

FISH: I'm prepared to change myself!
Anything he wants! I'll swing from the
chandeliers . . . I have done!

Pause. She walks about, smoking.

You know she threatened to kill herself.

DUSA: I know.

STAS *enters from work.*

FISH (*to* STAS): You know she threatened
to kill herself?

STAS: You told me.

FISH: Blackmail. Bloody blackmail.

STAS: We've got a woman on the wards
who tried it, stepped off the fourth floor
. . . broken pelvis and her face wired up.
For a feller? Forget it.

FISH: Oh, you're right, you're absolutely
right. He's still fallen for it, though.

STAS: You've spoken to him?

FISH: Yes.

STAS: Oh.

FISH: She's 'dependant'. She 'needs' him.
So . . . forget the struggle, forget politics
. . . on with the casseroled chicken – he's
walking about with pot plants under his
arm! – oh Christ, I can't fucking stop. We
went on and on on the phone . . . I
couldn't believe it was me saying all this
crap! I wouldn't let him ring off . . . I
couldn't bear it, I wanted to go on hearing

his voice. I only let him go by making him
promise to ring me again . . . poor bugger
didn't know whether he was coming or
going. I think I'll go to bed.

DUSA: Want anything?

FISH *shakes her head and goes.*

I wish I could be more support.

STAS: Stay out of it.

DUSA: All right for you, you're the only
one who's not in a mess.

STAS *gives her a dry look, unseen.*

People think Fish is OK because she hides
behind this sort of . . . you know, manner.

STAS: Mrs Pankhurst.

DUSA: Well, she could be in Acapulco,
sunning her feet. She doesn't have to get
involved.

STAS: Right.

DUSA: But she still does it. I admire that! I
admire people who are on the move.

STAS: Oh for God's sake, it's a breed! You
name it, they're up to their necks in it! I
had one once, against war or something
. . . she even had me signing! Next time we
met it was anti-fluoride and aerosols,
same spit all over me face. If it isn't
communes, it's astrology, tarot,
everything's down to the pyramids or
some guru . . . all the same bunch.

DUSA: Oh, that's shitty.

STAS: True.

DUSA: At least Fish puts her muscle where
her mouth is.

STAS: Fucking about.

DUSA: They're changing things!
Somebody's got to.

STAS: Why?

DUSA: Come on . . . we're not perfect yet.

STAS: I'll tell you what's changing things
. . . the last fifty years of physics and the
next fifty years of biology. What you're
talking about is fashion.

DUSA: Am I? No. The Russian revolution
wasn't fashion, that changed a few things.

STAS: Yeah. Check the body count.

DUSA: Science has casualty lists too, you
know.

STAS: Science is us, doing the best we can . . .

DUSA: So's Fish!

STAS: All right! Just so long as her little red book quotes the second law of thermo-dynamics.

DUSA: Eh?

STAS: That there is a tendency in the world for things to collapse. Ask my old Dad, back on the farm, he'll tell you.

DUSA (*slight pause*): Nonetheless . . . nonetheless, I do believe there are times in history . . . I mean, I can't talk about it like Fish . . .

STAS: Theory of great beauty, that . . . the second law.

DUSA: Oh, theories. I'm talking about people.

STAS (*slight pause*): We can replicate people now. Did you know that?

DUSA: What?

STAS: And we can cross-breed. A deer with a monkey . . . an elephant with a cow. Think about it. If you want an animal with rapid maturation . . . ready to eat in six weeks, with white flesh . . . and caviare . . . you've got it. Makes you think, eh? Fifty years from now we shan't need Concorde, we'll all have fins and feathers.

DUSA: Oh, come on.

STAS: True.

DUSA: Oh . . . well . . . I don't know anything about it.

STAS: No, that's the trouble with you lot. Back to brown rice and hope for the best.

DUSA: I worry about taking out the natural gas in case the sea falls in. Anyway . . . anyway . . . what about future shock?

STAS: We're due for that any minute. They're letting her out.

DUSA: Vi? When?

STAS: Today. She was going to discharge herself so they're sending her to a convalescent home –

VI (*enters*): They're not, you know. (*She puts down her tatty carrier bag.*) You didn't see that great big butch night sister, I thought she'd break me pelvis.

She gives STAS a noisy kiss.

STAS: Get off.

VI: I've got an affectionate nature, that's my trouble.

DUSA: Can't say I've noticed.

VI: Who's been messing up my things . . . look, it's all in a mess . . . and who's been wearing my Dockers?

DUSA: Do you mind?

STAS: Two days on hospital nosh and she's Hitler's best buddy.

VI: He was a very good tap dancer, few people know that.

FISH *enters from within. She is wearing a dress, jacket, and makeup. They look at her, startled, and she stares back, challenging.*

DUSA: Where are you going?

FISH: Out.

STAS: Your eye makeup's crooked.

FISH *opens the wardrobe, looks into the mirror on the back of the door, licks a finger and rubs.*

FISH: That better?

STAS: Not really.

FISH *rubs at her face again.*

FISH: Right. See you. (*She pauses a second.*) Right. (*She hovers uncertainly, then goes.*)

DUSA: Do something! (*To STAS:*) Go after her!

STAS: What?

DUSA: Go after her . . . follow her!

STAS: Who do you think I am, bloody Sam Spade . . . you follow her.

DUSA: I can't – I have to stay by the phone. Anyway, the TV people are ringing . . . they're coming to do an interview.

VI: With you? Are they?!

DUSA *groans.*

Wow!

STAS: Do you think she's gone off to do him in?

DUSA: Oh stop it. Aren't you going out tonight?

STAS: No . . got a discharge.

VI: Clap clinic?

STAS: Yup. Anyone for bean soup?

VI: Ooh, I've got some frozen curry and doughnuts. (*Leaping to her feet and dashing for the exit.*) Whatcha wanna drink . . . tea, coffee, gin?

DUSA ⎤
STAS ⎦ (*together*): Tea. Coffee.

VI: Right. (*She disappears.*)

STAS: What the hell have they given her?

The telephone rings. STAS *picks it up, answers, gives it to* DUSA.

DUSA: Thanks. Yes? Yes. Oh. No . . . no, I hadn't heard. Where . . . where? Oh, I see. (*She puts the telephone down carefully. Immediately it rings again. Quickly:*) No, Mrs Gilpin isn't here. (*She slams down the receiver.*)

STAS: Press again?

DUSA: It was the . . . the guy from the Telegraph. They're in Argentina.

There is a sudden flurry of movement from the two girls, a seeming scuffle. It becomes apparent that DUSA *is hysterical and out of control.* STAS *drags her away from the window.* DUSA *thrashes about making weird sounds, not like a human being.* STAS *hangs onto her, shouts for* VI, *who comes in and stands, paralysed.*

STAS: Get her bag, dammit.

VI *does so,* STAS *grabs it, takes out some pills,* VI *runs for a beaker of water and* STAS *forces* DUSA *to take tablets.* DUSA *does so, then stands, shivering. She sits down abruptly, still trembling violently.* VI *gets in the way, is shoved aside by* STAS, *who lifts* DUSA's *legs onto the sofa and covers her up with the old eiderdown.* DUSA *shakes under the cover.*

You'll be OK.

She sits, across from DUSA, *who continues to shake.*

(*To* VI:) Where's my grub?

VI (*hand to mouth*): Oh! Forgot.

STAS *looks at* DUSA, *who is beginning to subside, stands over her for a second, then lowers the lights and follows* VI *off.*

Music.

The next morning. DUSA *asleep. Bright morning sunshine.*
VI *enters. She has dressed herself up for cleaning. She switches on Capital Radio and begins spraying everything with aerosol polish, books as well. She makes a lot of noise, bopping to the music, and singing.*

DUSA (*jerks awake*): What? Oh. Christ. Shuddup!

VI: Oh, you're awake! Want some coffee? I know . . . glass of lemon juice . . . turns to alkali in the stomach.

DUSA: What?

VI: Good for you!

DUSA: Violet . . . what's the matter with you?

VI: I'm on these tablets. (*She rubs away, humming, galvanised.*)

DUSA *groans and sits up.*

Shan't be a tick, I'll fix you a tray, kettle's on . . . oooh! (*She dashes off.*)

DUSA *gets up, blunders about dopily, sits in alarm as* VI *surges back with a tray which she dumps on* DUSA's *lap.*

Lemon juice, muesli, yeast tablets, coffee and uppers . . . OK?

DUSA *nods submissively.* VI *sits cosily beside her.*

Right, what sort of scenario do you want?

DUSA *looks at her uncomprehendingly.*

For the TV . . . for the TV! Aren't they coming?

DUSA: What?

VI: To interview you . . . today!

DUSA: Oh. Oh God. Is it today . . . is today today?

VI: Look, are they going to interview all of us . . . or just you. I mean, do they need background material . . . human interest . . .

DUSA *laughs despite herself.*

DUSA: Oh, Violet . . .

VI: And listen, you gotta make a good impression. What about a suit . . . (*She bounds across to the armoire, pulls out a silk suit of* STAS's.) You can hitch it up with a belt . . . hey! Wow! What about this! (*She turns in triumph, displaying a fox fur, dyed ink-blue.*)

Look . . . fantastic! (*She drapes it about her neck.*)

DUSA: Violet, what do I want with a fox's bonce round my neck? (*She sips the lemon juice.*)

VI (*trying things on herself*): What you ought to have done was go home.

DUSA: Why?

VI: Be better. Then they could pan round the empty bedroom. Little shoe, just where it was dropped in the rush . . . teddy bear, lying on its side. I know! (*Making* DUSA *jump.*) A swing!

DUSA: What?

VI: A swing . . . a swing – have you got a swing? Get somebody to lend it you, then you could rig it up in the garden, do a shot of it swinging backwards and forwards . . . empty!

She waits for a response, standing over DUSA *in excitement.*

DUSA (*looks up*): If I went back there I'd kill myself.

VI: Oh. Right. Tch, still . . . you could get a lot of good ideas, you know.

She throws off her silly apron, fed up.

DUSA (*low*): Did Stas tell you they were in Argentina?

VI: Yeah. Still, it's very sunny there. (*She picks at food on the tray moodily.*)

DUSA: What time did Fish get in?

VI: Dunno, went to bed early. (*To* FISH, *who enters, wet, tired and bedraggled:*) Chr-ist, where have you been?

FISH (*mild*): You the fucking housemother or something?

VI: Only asked.

FISH: Bloody Puritan, that's what you are, old mate. (*She lights up.*)

DUSA: God, you're wet through! (*She helps* FISH *off with her clothes and gives her the purple kimono.*)

Where've you been, have you been out all night?

FISH: I watched them make love. From the fire escape.

Pause.

DUSA: What for?

FISH: We always left the curtains open . . . so I watched them.

DUSA: Fish!

FISH: Yeah, what a thing to do.

She shivers.

VI: What did they get up to?

FISH: Nothing much. She sauced about, waggling her head at him . . . I thought about hopping in and giving her a show. (*She groans.*) Oh . . . his lovely back!

STAS *enters, sleepy.*

VI: She spent all night on the fire escape watching them fuck.

FISH *and* STAS *exchange a brief glance.*

DUSA: Coffee?

FISH: Thanks. (*She takes the mug, drinks.*) She was wearing a flowered nightie and a little pearl necklace . . . the necklace stayed on – oh, I'm being bitchy! (*In genuine anguish.*)

DUSA: It sounds bloody awful.

FISH: Yes. I mean, I'm trying to wear it but . . . God, it was so banal! He called her my pet, they were giggling, both of them . . . like kids, pinching from Woolworths! I mean, I could stand his being undamaged . . . well, I couldn't . . . but after all, if he's happy . . . all right . . . but not this! He wants this? Shallow superficial snogging? After all the pain?

VI: Forget it. You wanna watch out for yourself, mate.

STAS: Right.

FISH (*to* STAS): OK.

STAS: I mean it. Because if you don't, somebody has to do it for you.

FISH: I'm not asking for help, I never have. I wouldn't dream of it.

STAS: No. Not your role, is it?

FISH: What's that supposed to mean?

VI (*quick*): So they didn't get up to much?

FISH: In and out like a yoyo, I couldn't believe it. Michelangelo, painting by numbers.

STAS: I don't know why you bother.

FISH: You think I should abandon him?

STAS: Look . . . the colony has seceded . . .

DUSA: Shut up.

STAS: . . . why not haul down the flag and tootle off?

DUSA: Stas!

STAS: What are you trying to do, restore law and order?

FISH: Oh yes! I know! My apologies for not having a pair of clogs over my bed. May I remind you that it was the despised middle classes who were called back to run Russia after the revolution.

STAS: Great job.

FISH: Oh, I didn't know you cared, I thought you were into the criminal culture. *I* shall get nicked for those coats, the flat's in my name!

STAS: What do you think you're doing? It's sick.

VI: Leave her alone.

STAS: Get the message – find another screw. What are you after, romantic love or something?

DUSA: Stas, leave it.

STAS: Walking the bloody boundaries – why don't you stick a fucking notice on him – trespassers will be shot!

DUSA: What did you do after they'd finished?

FISH: He came over to draw the curtains and saw me.

VI: What did he say?

FISH: He just looked furious, went over and turned out the light.

VI: Did he tell her?

FISH: No. They went to sleep – at least, one of them was sleeping, I could hear snoring. I expect it was her.

VI: You should have climbed in with them.

FISH: I thought about it. You can't open the window from the outside. I just sat in the rain looking out over London and wondering how many people were having their first screw.

STAS: Or their last.

VI: Urgh . . . ah! (*She mimes sudden death via orgasm.*)

FISH: I thought, if there was a flash of blue light . . . I wondered how many there'd be. Green if they were in love, red for rape. I'm going to bed. (*She goes.*)

A pause.

STAS: Blue flashes!

DUSA: Oh, leave it.

VI: I reckon she's making it up.

STAS: Do you? (*Unconvinced.*)

DUSA: No, Fish never tells lies.

The telephone rings. DUSA *picks it up absently.*

Yes? Yes, speaking. Yes . . . yes – what? Oh no . . . no! Oh, it's – yes! . . . no, no . . . no . . . yes . . . oh thank you! Yes, I see. Yes. Thank you. Yes . . . right, then . . . yes. I'll be here – oh, and thank you! Thank you . . . oh! (*She puts down the telephone.*) They know where they are. And they're alive.

VI: Why? Did you think they were dead?

DUSA (*quietly*): Yes. (*She collapses into a chair, closes her eyes briefly.*) Yes, I thought they were dead. I've been thinking they were dead.

Pause.

(*Quietly:*) You don't understand.

You love them too much. It's unbearable. From the moment they're born. The way they look – they're beautiful . . . oh never mind if they're good looking or not. Your bowels are never still. They're late. Was it a lorry . . . a man in a mac? Polio . . . meningitis . . . (*A brief laugh.*) Hostages to fortune for the rest of your bloody life. I mean, they can let go when they're ready. You can't. (*She shrugs.*) You're just an old balloon after the party. Of course, nowadays . . . big deal . . . you can retrain . . . become a computer data programmer . . . see life. No, it's a tough act to follow, I tell you. (*A small pause. Then a thought strikes her.*) Oh my God, Frank! He'll be in a terrible state!

STAS: Fuck him.

DUSA: Don't be such a fascist! Things aren't all cause and effect, crime and punishment, you win I lose. Sodding easy if it were.

STAS: Where did you spring from? (*She grins, goes.*)

DUSA (*calls after her*): I'm not entirely lacking in consciousness!

We hear STAS *laugh, off.*

Do you want to see their pictures?

VI: Look, don't make me sick, I'm on uppers at the mo.

DUSA: Oh Vi, you're a freak.

She hugs VI, *who gives her a big, wet, open-mouthed kiss.* DUSA *giggles.*

DUSA (*vamping*): Who d'you like best, boys or girls?

VI: Both. (*Darkly*:) Well, depends on me mood.

DUSA (*capering wildly*): They're alive!!!

Lights down.

Music link.

Lights up. DUSA *wanders on, is drawn to the wardrobe, tries on a couple of* STAS's *things, keeps one on. She goes. Fade.*

Music link.

Fade up on FISH, *reading,* DUSA *enters, looking good.*

DUSA: Hi . . . want anything?

FISH *smiles, shakes her head.*

I was going to make some coffee and a club sandwich.

FISH: No, I've had something.

DUSA: Oh, right. When?

FISH: Just now. In the kitchen.

DUSA: Oh, but I thought – OK.

FISH (*smiles*): Stop humouring me, damn you.

A slight pause.

DUSA: Is that why you've only been speaking to Stas?

FISH: I'm sorry, I didn't mean to upset you.

DUSA: That's all right. (*Pause.*)

FISH: Only I get the notion that you're keeping an eye on me. It's unnerving.

DUSA: Sorry.

FISH: That's all right. It's just that when I think you're trying to . . . look after me, it gives me ugly thoughts.

DUSA: What do you mean?

FISH: It makes me feel that you're trying to climb on my face.

DUSA: I don't know what you mean.

FISH: No, well, that's because I'm being hateful.

A pause.

Did I tell you I met them, on the street?

DUSA: Who?

FISH (*patient*): Alan and his woman. They asked me to dinner.

A pause.

DUSA: There's no answer to that.

FISH *laughs.* DUSA *giggles and they both begin to laugh helplessly. They roll about, laughing . . . subside, then start again. At last the laughing gives way to a thoughtful silence. Pause.*

FISH: Well, go on.

DUSA: What do you mean?

FISH: With the pronouncement. I can hear the wheels grinding.

DUSA: Oh God, bad as that?

FISH: Let me think. I should . . . take a holiday . . . a lover . . . a running jump?

DUSA: You could stop being so remorselessly bright, it's wearing us all down.

FISH: But I feel bright! No . . . really, I'm full of hilarity, I surprise myself. And worry not, little mother. I have met a dark stranger, as the tealeaves foretold.

DUSA: You devil! From the raight backgranhnd I trust?

FISH: Honesht, shober . . . and nevver wivaht is flat 'at.

DUSA: Do you mean it?

FISH: Of course I mean it.

DUSA: Good.

FISH: Why, what's the matter?

DUSA: Just thought you might be doing your noble patrician . . . letting us off the hook.

FISH (*very irritable*): Oh for Christ's sake! (*She goes, slamming the door.*)

Music link.

Lights up on DUSA and VI, playing chess.

VI: Check . . . and mate.

DUSA: You've picked this up fast.

FISH (*enters, from without*): Hullo, loves, how's it going, I need a clean shirt, I've been working the press. (*She comes and goes, changing.*)

VI: She spoke to the kids on the phone.

FISH: No . . . marvellous . . . any more news?

DUSA: They're going to ring. What are you doing?

FISH (*with an armful of leaflets*): I'm going to drop these off, then I'm going over to Fulham to do an interview with two tin miners from Bolivia . . . and then I'm going to meet my young man for a beer and a wad . . . Chinese meal, actually. After that I'm going back to the press.

DUSA: Need any help there?

FISH: Could you, love? . . . any time. (*She goes.*)

STAS *enters. She throws down her stack of airtickets, on the table between the two girls.*

STAS: What do you think of that? Hawaii. Hardly dented the roll, I know a feller on the airline. (*She sighs with relief.*) No more appointments after this month. Only two quickies tonight, I'll be back in time for the serial – what time's it on?

VI (*rolling and lighting a smoke*): Half-past nine.

STAS: Right. I'm off. (*But she slumps. Pause.*)

VI: You better get washed.

STAS (*louche*): Oh fuck it.

VI: Right, I'll have a bath, then. (*She leaves the smoke with STAS and goes.*)

A pause.

STAS: Funny really. I've always thought my mother a rather boring woman.

A pause.

DUSA: Do you think I could get a flat around here?

STAS: Are you joking?

She hands the joint to DUSA. DUSA plays idly with the travel tickets.

(*After a pause.*) There's a place at home I always go to . . . dunno why. Near a great big turkey oak. It's not worth anything, the wood's no good. There's part of an old iron gate there, with some dead convolvulus . . . been there ever since we were kids. A dog got its head stuck through it once. Quite nice in the spring. A few primroses. I don't know why . . . it's not pretty or anything. (*Her voice breaks slightly.*)

DUSA: Stas . . . what's the matter . . . what are you crying for?

STAS: Rubbish, I'm fine.

She gets up, gives the joint to DUSA, crosses to the wardrobe, throws off her sweater . . . she is wearing nothing underneath. She makes to find something to wear, can't be bothered and slips a fur coat over her trousers and bare torso and goes, quietly.

Music link.

Crossfade lights. Up on VI *and* DUSA. FISH *enters.*

DUSA (*sleepy*): Hi.

VI: How was the food?

FISH: Not bad. Went back to his place after.

DUSA ⎤ (*together*): How was it?
VI ⎦ Any good?

FISH: Super-duper, Gary Cooper.

VI: I told you.

FISH: And you were right. An excellent young man.

She disappears into the bedroom for a moment.

DUSA: Do you believe it?

VI: Sure, why not . . . don't you?

DUSA: Sure.

FISH *returns.*

Sorry I didn't come down to the press.

FISH: I'm not there either. Yow!

DUSA: Tired?

FISH: I'm exhausted.

VI: She's falling in love!

FISH: That I might, if somebody'd let me off the bloody hook.

DUSA: Who . . . Alan?

FISH: The bugger's even following me around. I went to Ryman's to get some staples, there he was. Same in the supermarket, same at the wholesaler's. Took a bus to Shepherd's Bush . . . who should be following in the red car . . . it's ridiculous!

DUSA: Fish, are you sure?

FISH: Of course I'm sure. He was in the pub tonight . . . well, no reason why he shouldn't be in the pub, he usually is.

VI: Funny though.

DUSA: Doesn't make sense.

FISH: God, I'm tired.

DUSA *rises, goes.* VI *leaves, separately.* FISH, *alone, crosses to music centre, puts on a cassette. She returns, sits. She listens, flopped, without expression . . . gets up and leaves before the end of the song.*

Music link.

Lights up on STAS *and* VI *decorating the coffee table with garlands and large paper flowers.*
STAS *goes to wardrobe, takes out a cake in a box to show to* VI.

STAS: Mocha sponge with pistachio icing . . . great huh? What's the matter?

VI: I was going to make one for her!

STAS: I'll believe you. Were you? Oh. Sorry. (*She puts the cake back in the wardrobe.*)

VI: I don't know what to get her now.

STAS: Give her some of your stash. (VI *pulls a face.*) Oh . . . by the way. She's pregnant.

VI: Who?

STAS: Alan Duncan's woman.

VI: Ooh.

STAS: Don't say anything.

VI: No. Right.

The telephone rings. They lock stares. VI *loses and answers the telephone.*

Yup? Uhuh. Uhuh. Uhuh. Okeydoke. Yup, I'll tell her. (*She slams down the phone, sucks her teeth, returns to her task.*)

STAS: That it?

VI (*mock American accent*): They are putting them on thee plane.

STAS: Thank God for that. (*She arranges the flowers to her satisfaction.*) You fancy having kids?

VI: Me? Yich!

STAS: Yeah, me too . . . weird.

DUSA *enters, breathless.*

DUSA: Hullo!

VI ⎤ (*together, silly voices*): Hellew!
STAS ⎦

DUSA: Somebody rang!

VI: Yeah.

DUSA: Was it for me?

STAS: Tell 'er!

VI: I was going to! What you getting so
worried about?

DUSA: They've got them!

VI: Yup.

DUSA: Oh! What did they say . . . what did
they say?

VI: Well . . . like they said . . . is Mrs Gilpin
here . . . I said . . .

They scream at her.

They're putting them on a plane, you
gotta be at London Airport tomorrow
morning, they'll ring back with the details
soon as they get them.

DUSA *screams and laughs and goes into a
wild, capering dance. The other two join
in, kicking up their legs like demented
marionettes.*

VI (*suddenly remembering*): Hey . . . you
know Fish's feller –

STAS: Vi!

VI: – that Alan – his bird's expecting.

STAS: Vi!

DUSA: Oh no.

VI: Yup. Having a kid.

DUSA: Violet, are you sure?

STAS: Apparently.

DUSA: Oh. They could have waited.

STAS: Free country.

VI: We're not going to say anything.

DUSA: Right.

FISH *enters.*

VI (*quick*): She's got the kids!

FISH: What?! Ah! (*She embraces* DUSA.)

DUSA: Tomorrow! They're going to ring
me.

FISH: Oh, my love . . . marvellous. I was
beginning to think I was bad luck . . . we
must celebrate!

STAS *and* VI *move aside, revealing the
decorated table.*

STAS: Tara!

VI: For your birthday.

FISH: For me?

VI (*to* DUSA): Did you get the balloons?
(*They all blow up balloons.*) I like
balloons.

FISH (*to* DUSA): We'll go to the toyshop.
(*She laughs.*) Last year Alan and I spent
the day on the river. It pissed with rain so
we got drunk, and all the buggers in the
pub said was talk about ways of doing
yourself in. Apparently if you take whisky
you throw up . . . red wine's the thing.

STAS (*to* VI): Hey, Skin . . . coming to the
pictures?

VI: OK.

*She lets go the balloon she has been
inflating, crosses.* STAS *holds out one of
her fur coats,* VI *cuddles into it, and
sashays off on* STAS's *arm. The other two
watch, amazed.*

DUSA: She's going out. I don't believe it!

FISH (*mock-American*): It's the
medication, baby. (*Ordinary voice.*) Oh,
she'll piddle about, changing seats . . . has
to be the end of a row of course.

DUSA: Yes . . . I get claustrophobia.

FISH: So do we all love, name of the game.
(*She sits, displaying exhaustion.*)

DUSA: You OK?

FISH: Sure. (*A slight pause.*) He's still
doing it, you know.

DUSA: What?

FISH: Following me around.

DUSA: Alan? Fish, are you sure?

A pause.

FISH: Bloody nerve.

DUSA: Tell him to stop.

FISH: Oh, he knows I won't do that. He
knows this boy I'm with's just the time of
day –

DUSA: Fish, for God's sake –

FISH: Don't worry! The guy's in a mess,
Dusa! The least I can do is stay cool . . .
lay off while he works it out. It's not
serious.

DUSA: They are married.

FISH *gives her a look of amused scorn.*

What I'm saying is, she could get
pregnant.

FISH: No. No, no. Not in a million years.

DUSA: He might not know.

FISH: He's not that irresponsible!

DUSA: But if she – look, he might not be able to prevent it –

FISH: Love, you don't understand. He knows what it would do to me. He's not a cunt.

DUSA: I'm just saying, suppose she lets him think she's on the pill and then tells him when it's too late – it could happen.

FISH: Not to Alan. He'd leave her. He wouldn't wear that. No, give the poor cow her due, she won't piss on her own chips.

DUSA: Well, I wouldn't trust her.

FISH: I trust him! Oh I know he's said some nasty things . . . about being fed up with me . . . the pain . . . but that's not what it's all about. We're breaking moulds together. Not easy.

DUSA: He's always been ambitious.

FISH (*surprised*): Alan? I suppose so. For the right things. We both are. It's just that when you're working on the point of the arrow – the rim . . . it's tiring. We'll make it. We have to. Otherwise . . . (*She takes DUSA's hand.*) Look at you, love. There's got to be a new deal for us . . . none of the either/or, 'You, too, can have a career and five abortions in the name of progress'. That's a fashion I'll leave out. We have to break new ground. Together.

DUSA: He didn't have to marry her.

FISH: We were tired! She must have seemed like a rest – anyway, I ran off with Pete Loudon, we were both off our heads.

DUSA (*slight pause*): You think he'd leave her if she got pregnant?

FISH: Hope to God she doesn't, Alan won't fall into that moralistic trap, thank you very much, I know him too well.

DUSA (*slight pause*): Suppose she does herself in?

FISH: She won't.

DUSA: She might.

FISH: She won't!

DUSA: How do you know?

FISH: Because I know . . . I know!

DUSA: All right . . . all right.

FISH: I know.

DUSA (*after a pause*): How do you know?

FISH: I know, that's all.

DUSA (*after a pause*): I worry about you.

FISH: Don't. (*A slight pause.*) There's no need. Believe me – anyway, you've got your own worries. What will you do?

DUSA: Sorry?

FISH: What's going to happen?

DUSA: I'll be OK . . . I'll get a job. I'll be fine.

FISH: Sure. You always did have your feet on the ground. God I'm tired. You know, I've even thought *I* might be pregnant.

DUSA (*slight pause*): Probably the weather.

FISH: Sure. (*A slight pause.*) I think I'll kip.

She grins companionably at DUSA, rolls over onto the divan. DUSA crosses, flips a cover over her, turns out the light and goes.

Pause in black.

STAS *and* VIOLET *enter on tiptoe, drunk, using a torch in order not to disturb. They do not notice that it is* FISH *in bed. Giggling, they cross to the wardrobe, taking off their coats.* STAS *puts two bottles of wine on the decorated coffee table, ready for the birthday party.*

VI (*at the wardrobe*): Hey . . . did I tell you? I've got a job.

STAS: You're joking.

VI: I'm not. Start tomorrow. Shift work. Hey . . . shift work!

They begin to laugh again. STAS *falls back into the armoire among the coats.*

STAS: Oh fuck.

VI: What?

STAS: I've sat on the cake.

She gets up, tries to take VI's *coat, but* VI *resists and keeps it on. They cross, going.*

VI: Who's going to the airport tomorrow . . . ?

STAS: With the earth mother? You are! (*Convulsed by her own wit.*) I know . . . I know . . . why don't we all go? Get your picture taken! (*And laughs as* VI's *face brightens, then sags as she realises she is being mocked.*)

VI: Wouldn't mind making a day of it.

STAS: Oh, good . . . right . . . you're on.

They go. . . . STAS *singing 'Bali Hi'.*

Half light.

DUSA *enters fully dressed.*

DUSA: Fish, are you coming . . . (*She shakes her gently.*) Fish?

STAS *stumbles on with a hangover.*

STAS (*groans*): Oh, God.

DUSA: Come on, there isn't time. We'll leave her presents so's she can see them when she wakes up. Vi . . . Vi, are you coming? Sssh, don't wake her.

VI *enters wearing a traffic warden's uniform.*

STAS: I don't believe it.

VI: Don't worry, I'll see the sods off . . . I hate cars.

STAS: I don't believe it.

DUSA: Come on! (*She puts her present by the bed.*) Happy birthday, love.

STAS *leaves a small present, follows* DUSA *off.* VI *makes out a ticket, puts it under* FISH's *pillow together with a small parcel.*

VI: Happy birthday, kid.

She bounds out after the others.

Blackout.

Lights up. STAS *enters, humming. She is carrying a child's toy.*

FISH *is lying half out of bed.*
STAS *stops, then hurls herself across the room. She kneels, turns* FISH *over, pushes open an eye. She feels for a pulse, listens for a heartbeat.*

DUSA (*off*): Mind the stairs, Bennie . . .

STAS: Keep those kids out of here . . . out!

DUSA *enters. She sees* FISH . . . *backs and turns, runs out to the children.*

STAS *pinches the back of* FISH's *leg, for response. She feels for a pulse again.*
VI *enters.* STAS *looks up . . . indicates the empty wine bottles.*
VI *stands, paralysed.*

DUSA *returns.*

STAS, *after listening again for a heartbeat, drops* FISH's *hand, and brushes the hair back from* FISH's *forehead briefly. She rises . . . looks about . . . finds two empty bottles of pills. And a note.*

STAS (*reads*): 'Oh my loves, I'm so sorry. I seem to have lost the knack of it. How could I have got it so wrong. I thought there was understanding. I thought we were getting somewhere. There's no love, and I can't face the thought of fighting . . . forgive me. It's hard. I wanted so much to sit under a tree with my children and there doesn't seem to be a place for that any more, and I feel cheated. I've been seething with it for more than two years, but now I'm tired and it's not important any more. I don't feel fertile any more.

'Please try and explain to my mother. I know it will be hard for her to understand because she stuck it out. Tell her that I love her most particularly, and that I've always remembered the lovely days in Felixstowe, whenever I've been low. We've been apart, but not really.

'See Alan for me. Tell him not to grieve. He couldn't come with me and there it is. Perhaps in the end we do have to fight. But I don't want that. I never have. It's not right . . . not for me. I've been seeing him everywhere.

'My loves, what are we to do? We won't do as they want any more, and they hate it. What are we to do?'

Dusa, Fish, Stas and Vi

I wrote this play, under the title of *Dead Fish*, in 1974, after finishing *Piaf* (which was not produced until 1978, when it was done by the RSC and subsequently on Broadway). I wanted to try a contemporary play, and to try to write in 'takes', since I felt that most of us, being reared on film and television, responded in a synaptic way to material nowadays. I felt, or rather hoped that it was possible to convey information, a climate, in condensed 'fragments'. I was also influenced by the composer, Paul Sand, who was living on the floor below with a six piece band; and there was a fine woman singer, Barbara Jung. The idea was that the writing would be dry and light and surface, and that songs would carry the emotion. This production played the Edinburgh Festival in 1976, under the direction of Caroline Eves. In the autumn of the same year Nancy Meckler mounted a new production at the Hampstead Theatre under a new title (it was felt that the original title was a giveaway) and this version successfully used radio clips instead of the songs to give distance and objectivity . . . one saw the girls' lives as under a microscope. The play transferred to the Mayfair Theatre, where it had a successful run which ended when Brigit Forsyth, who played Dusa, was eight months pregnant.

To my surprise, the piece aroused some controversy, because of the suicide of the political activist, Fish. It was felt, by some people, that this was a slur on the left, and that the play was thereby bourgeois and individualistic. The 'depressive' ending struck the wrong political note. I am not a writer of polemic, which I believe belongs on the platform. The play has two themes, Fish the pathfinder . . . the woman attempting to break out a new, equitable way of living . . . and finding resistance . . . and Fish the upper-class woman who can give help but who is unable to receive it. It seemed to me when I was writing the play that for all the rhetoric, and the equal opportunities, and the Sex Discrimination Acts, that society had not moved one step towards accommodating the other fifty per cent of us and our needs. Not that the age of industry fires the imagination of any of us too much, men or women. But to be told, as women, that we were to be allowed to 'join', as fully fledged citizens was one thing. How we were supposed to do it, and breed and rear our young, particularly in a country which since the war had chosen to build offices and high-rises rather than houses where people might live in some sort of dignity and privacy – well, we've seen the result of all that. The crux of the play, for me, was the Rosa Luxemburg speech. To some extent I modelled Fish on her, since Rosa was a middle-class woman who took the path of socialism. And took it in a head-on fashion. And gave her life for it. Perhaps, in the end, we have to choose devious compromise, if that is the price of survival . . . in a way the extreme is always too easy. However, I now think that the reason for Fish's decision not to live was the failure of love. The antagonism between the sexes has been painful, an indictment of our age. It is true that many women have been drawn, properly, to the Women's Movement after abuse by bad husbands, fathers . . . they have had hopes pushed aside, seeing brothers favoured from infancy. It makes for grievance, fear and resentment. But, as often, one sees men hopelessly damaged by women . . . their mothers. We cannot separate ourselves. Many of us know that all we have, as Gandhi said, against the hardware, is the strength of our spirits . . . and love. One of his main reasons for advocating non-violence was that it could be practised by everyone. Thus, he said, women and children and the old were as potent as the strongest man. Fish had tried for a new, sharing life with her lover. He didn't want it . . . he felt better off in a traditional relationship. And she couldn't, wouldn't fight.

It's an interesting point. The argument has been put that by not allowing women to fight, men are able to romanticise war into gallantry and protection. I wonder. I was horrified in America to hear disguised advertisements on the radio 'saluting our gals in the armed services'. True, there was a recent veto on the bearing of arms by women . . . though many women believe that it is their responsibility to fight alongside the men if we are to be fully paid-up members of society. Well, in the first place, it isn't our society. It isn't made at all in our image. Women have spent the first part of their history peopling the world. Only recently have we begun to emerge from the hazards of that – think of all the widowers in Victorian novels. Are we to take on board without question the Roman notions of property, territory and the ethics of trade, competition, and high consumption? Is it in our nature? What is our nature? In any case, isn't it enough that half the world bears arms? Must the other half join in without question? I, myself, feel that there is something deeply criminal and dangerous in women who fight. We *make* the arms and legs and torsos. We *make* the bodies, we invest a good deal of our lives in it. Men are programmed to range, defend and protect. We are not, not in the same way. Aggression in woman is an existential act, except in the direct defence of her young. Fish does not want a fight. Not in the name of love. And without love she dies.

Several years after the play was first written it is disheartening to see so little progress on behalf, in particular, of women writers in the theatre. Our history is just beginning. Women are talking to women . . . it's the first time there's been the leisure for us, we're beginning to be on our own feet, and no longer reduced to the spiteful rivalry of the 'wife of'. A good deal of work is being done, in literature, and in research. But there are not many plays . . . at least, very few produced. Why is this? There are a number of reasons.

First, playwriting is done alone. There are no formal courses, thus, you emerge without colleagues (unless you are an actor or have worked elsewhere in the theatre). The theatre is a closed world. It is hard to get in. Because it deals with the imagination, and the concomitant 'glamour' and 'fame', it attracts a lot of people. There is power . . . artistic directors and producers become corrupted. All theatres receive a lot of playscripts. The logistics are impossible. So you have some sort of system of farming out plays to readers . . . often little more than a show. And just as the critics exist to make their fame and fortune, not yours, so directors live, not to serve art . . . well, I've met few who do, or who even understand it. They want success. If you are an artist, you have to find, first, a way to work – time, enough money to eat . . . peace and quiet. You have to acquire, develop and refine your own craft. You are, by nature, obsessive, perfectionist. And you put the best of yourself into the work. You have to be wet and open. For the work. Which means, if you're any good at all, that you're useless against the hustlers. When you emerge with your work, you're ill-equipped to sell it. You are not 'in' the theatre . . . the quality of your work depends on your staying out of it. To use the popular quote from *The Merchant,* you bring the news from the Rialto.

It is a difficult dilemma. And worse for women since, apart from time taken rearing children, women have few positions of power in the theatre. They don't have the pub, club network which is so important in making those awful 'connections'. I've seen people working at this sort of thing, and it is effective. But it kills you. It kills truthful work. To be blunt, in an over-crowded profession, you are on your own. There are few who will help – you are, in fact, a threat. There seems to be invitation – from time to time, play competitions . . . invitations to join playreading or workshop groups. But the former are, in my opinion, hateful, invoking the animus. And a lot of workshops are a wank or a fiddle, a bit of gravy-training within the theatre. There is only one way to learn the craft, and that is to write a play, and then get it performed before a live audience.

It doesn't get any easier. You have to push in somehow, find the energy and courage to take the snubs and rejections, and stand by the work. This means you have to believe in the work. Which means putting it first, and that's hard, if you have a family. But only if you know what you want to say, and need passionately to say it, does the courage come to stick it out. Which is as it should be. Art is of necessity. Which is why we need women playwrights just now very badly. We have our own history to create, and to write. Personally, I think there will be brilliant women playwrights. I think the form suits us. Women are very funny, coarse, subversive. All good qualities for drama, and for the achievement of progress by the deployment, not of violence, but of subtlety, love and imagination.

Pam Gems

PAM GEMS

Stage Plays

Betty's Wonderful Christmas (Cockpit Theatre 1972). Play for children and adults.

My Warren, After Birthday (Sandra) (Almost Free Theatre 1973).

The Amiable Courtship of Miz Venus and Wild Bill (Almost Free Theatre 1974).

Go West, Young Woman (Roundhouse 1974).

Up in Sweden (Haymarket, Leicester 1975).

My Name is Rosa Luxemburg (translation from Marianne Auricoste: Soho Poly 1976).

The Rivers and Forests (translation from Duras: Soho Poly 1976).

The Project (Soho Poly 1976).

Dead Fish (later *Dusa, Fish, Stas and Vi*: Edinburgh Festival 1976).

Guinevere (Edinburgh Festival 1976).

Queen Christina (Royal Shakespeare Company, The Other Place 1977).

Piaf (Royal Shakespeare Company, The Other Place 1978).

Uncle Vanya (new version of Chekhov play: Hampstead Theatre Club 1979).

A Doll's House (new version of Ibsen play: Tyne/Wear 1980).

TISSUE

Tissue was first presented at the Studio Theatre of the Belgrade, Coventry on 3 May 1978, with the following cast:

SALLY	Elizabeth Revil
MAN	Michael Cassidy
WOMAN	Kate Crutchley

Directed by Nancy Diuguid
Designed by James Helps
Stage manager Joanne Richler-Ostroff

One

SALLY: Why me? It is a question as unsolvable as why I am here? Why me?

MAN: It has to happen to someone you know.

WOMAN: All this fuss over a pound of flesh.

MAN: It's not a functional organ after all.

WOMAN: If you don't want children, why do you need a breast?

MAN: God moves in mysterious ways.

WOMAN: It's not as if you're married.

MAN: It's only a bit of tissue.

WOMAN: Did you ever notice that you had it in the first place?

MAN: Put a bit of cotton wool in it.

WOMAN: Don't talk about it here.

MAN: If it hadn't been you it would have been someone else.

SALLY: But it is me. And I am here.

Two

SALLY: I'm wearing knickers, in bed.

MAN: You'll have to get yourself some frillies.

SALLY: Said doctor, pulling my gown up and the sheets down.

WOMAN: Can you get a friend to bring you in some briefs?

SALLY: Said sister, pulling my gown down and the sheets up.

So my mother sent me undies, first class, still in their bag without their bill.

So the problem of decency under the sheets is resolved. I've got knickers on.

MAN: You'll have to get yourself a nightie and a housecoat.

SALLY: This isn't mine. You've lost mine.

WOMAN: Can you manage that? Ask a friend to bring them in?

SALLY: I haven't got one.

And am so confused I don't know if I mean a nightie, a housecoat or a friend.

WOMAN: What do you wear?

SALLY: Nothing!

MAN: Pardon?

SALLY: He is as surprised as if I said I went to the door in my birthday suit.

Nothing!

WOMAN: What do you do if someone comes to the front door?

SALLY: Nothing!

MAN: Or the back?

SALLY: Nothing!

WOMAN: What?

SALLY: Nothing!

WOMAN: Oh!

SALLY: I don't answer. Not early in the morning.

Three

WOMAN: Miss Bacon, Miss Bacon, time to wake up.

SALLY: What time is it?

WOMAN: Seven.

SALLY: Every morning here at seven, because they shake me to make me face the day –

WOMAN: Wakey, wakey, Miss Bacon –

SALLY: And do not allow me to slip back, not even to semi-fantasy, I see the shimmer of purple and green sea nylon with lace billows of the bathroom rush. In case someone rips the sheets from them and shoves a towel under and lathers.

I smell.

WOMAN: Not at all, you don't.

SALLY: The nurse of course, denies it. They have to. But I stink.

WOMAN: We'll get every bit of you as clean as a new pin.

SALLY: In spite of perfect hygiene techniques, I am stronger than all the cleanliness put about me. More pungent than mattress disinfectant and –

WOMAN: Is this the talc I'm to use?

SALLY: Yes. Do I smell?

WOMAN: Yes. You're a blue gardenia!

Four

WOMAN: Sally!

SALLY: What?

WOMAN: Sally, don't!

SALLY: What, Mum?

WOMAN: Do that.

SALLY: I'm washing myself.

WOMAN: Not like that though.

SALLY: Like what?

WOMAN: If you want to wash your – your chest – do it with your flannel. Put the soap on your flannel and then use your flannel.

SALLY: It's much quicker if you just put the soap on with your hands. If you do it like this it's much better.

WOMAN: Don't, Sally!

SALLY: Simon does!

WOMAN: Simon might. But that's different. Ladies don't.

SALLY: Does Dad? Does he put the soap on a flannel first? Or does he just put it straight on?

WOMAN: Sally, don't wash your face with that flannel. Not when you've used it there. That's a smelly thing to do.

Five

SALLY: Do I smell?

WOMAN: That will pass.

SALLY: They say and –

WOMAN: Have another squirt of spray –

SALLY: Which mostly misses and stales on the sheets. It is true.

WOMAN: Of course she smells. The wound is septic. I try not to breathe in through my nose but through my mouth and have to keep swallowing more than I should because the saliva is flowing from the ducts of my mouth and drowning my tongue between my jaws. She has an infection in her wound which will swell with pus and burst.

Six

SALLY: A spurt. A dab behind the ears, on the wrists, the neck, behind the knees and between the breasts –

Don't!

MAN: Come on.

SALLY: Don't!

MAN: Sally?

SALLY: Don't!

MAN: Come on.

SALLY: Don't touch me.

MAN: God, you're tense.

SALLY: Don't touch me.

MAN: Why?

SALLY: I don't want you to.

MAN: So what's wrong?

SALLY: I don't know.

Pause.

You can't feel anything, can you? Not a lump?

MAN: Where?

SALLY: There.

MAN: There? In your tit?

SALLY: In my bosom. Is there a lump there?

MAN: You've knocked yourself somewhere.

SALLY: I know I haven't. I'd remember if I had.

MAN: Why?

SALLY: Come on. It's obvious.

MAN: Okay. You're not bruised. You didn't hit yourself hard.

SALLY: I know I didn't. Can you feel a lump?

MAN: If you haven't knocked yourself there can't be anything.

SALLY: I don't want to be told there's nothing. I want you to check that there isn't.

MAN: You do it.

SALLY: Why me?

MAN: It's your tit.

SALLY: I don't know what it's supposed to feel like.

MAN: Suppose I do?

SALLY: You bloody well ought to. You're the one who touches them.

MAN: Go to the doctor in the morning. Now come on.

SALLY: Go to the doctor?

MAN: Ask him to feel you.

SALLY: God, you're callous.

MAN: Get him to examine you.

SALLY: But he won't know.

MAN: They feel hundreds.

SALLY: But not mine. Please. I want to know if I've got a lump.

MAN: Don't get hysterical.

SALLY: I want you to tell me.

MAN: Okay.

SALLY: What if I have?

MAN: You know why it happens? Because frigid women want it to. There's nothing there.

SALLY: Isn't there?

MAN: No.

SALLY: Are you sure?

MAN: There? Feel. There's nothing.

SALLY: No. Perhaps it's muscular.

Seven

WOMAN: As Sally's mother I watched her changing and becoming a woman. Her body taking on contours. I watched her as her body tried to copy mine as I had tried to copy my mother's. I watched her as she began to look in the mirror closely. Then –

Sally?

SALLY: What, Mum?

WOMAN: Can I come in?

SALLY: No.

WOMAN: Only quickly. I want a vest for Simon.

SALLY: No.

WOMAN: Come on, Sally. Why not?

SALLY: It's engaged.

WOMAN: Why?

SALLY: I've formed.

Eight

SALLY: Doctor, I smell.

MAN: Of course. You've got an infection. If you were an animal you would have licked yourself to rid yourself of the smell, thus keeping the wound free from infection. Very crafty, nature. But we've invented antiseptics now. Very clever, men.

SALLY: In former days he would have come to me, knowing of my wound, drawn to it with the same power as a hound on the scent of a fox, but not to tear me to pieces but to lick me clean.

MAN: Or any animal of the flock would have come, as ready as the others and as willing with its tongue.

SALLY: Or I would have licked myself alone.

Nine

SALLY: At school we were taught –

WOMAN: If you prick your finger and get blood on your sewing, the only way to take out the mark is to spit on your finger, a clean finger – then rub the mark with your spittle until it goes.

SALLY: In needlework we made cookery aprons and nightdresses.

MAN: Can you get a nightie?

SALLY: Said doctor.

It was brushed cotton, pink, with sprigs of yellow flowers and blue ribbons. My mother's still using it for cleaning rags. She's been using it for rags since –

WOMAN: Sally is not neat.

SALLY: Appeared on my report. The end of term had come and I was still taking out –

WOMAN: Those tacking stitches because they are too large and not straight.

SALLY: I gave up domestic arts for language. A surgeon is a man who must like cutting and stitching.

Ten

WOMAN: Can I help you?

SALLY: I want to see the doctor.

WOMAN: Yes? Name?

SALLY: Bacon.

WOMAN: As in egg?

SALLY: Yes.

WOMAN: And the initials?

SALLY: S.

WOMAN: Wait here.

SALLY: Thank you.

WOMAN: Forename?

SALLY: Sally.

WOMAN: Is that short for Sarah?

SALLY: No. It's my name.

WOMAN: And the surname?

SALLY: Bacon. As in egg.

WOMAN: Thank you.

We've not got a card for you. Are you registered here?

SALLY: Pardon?

WOMAN: Have you seen a doctor here before?

SALLY: Here? No.

WOMAN: Well, no wonder I can't find a card for you. If you're not a patient you should have said. Are you a temporary?

SALLY: What?

WOMAN: Are you in the district temporarily?

SALLY: How long is temporary?

WOMAN: Will you be in the district for longer than three months?

SALLY: I don't know.

WOMAN: Umh –

SALLY: Please, can I register?

WOMAN: Yes – well, I'll give you a temporary form to fill in. Is it an emergency?

SALLY: An emergency?

WOMAN: Doctor doesn't have to take you on unless it's an emergency.

SALLY: I'm not sure.

WOMAN: What are your symptoms?

SALLY: I've – are you a nurse?

WOMAN: Not trained but I've picked up a lot working here.

SALLY: I have to see a doctor.

WOMAN: Doctor doesn't have to treat you unless it's an emergency.

SALLY: But I need to see one.

WOMAN: I should try another practice.

SALLY: But –

WOMAN: Why don't you try a couple of aspirins and a day in bed with a hot water bottle? You don't need a sick note for a day.

SALLY: I don't want a sick note. I want a proper physical examination.

WOMAN: The doctors here are very busy people. I wouldn't trouble them unless it's really necessary.

SALLY: Where do I find another doctor. Where do you recommend?

WOMAN: The doctors here are very good.

SALLY: Where do I find a surgery.

WOMAN: How did you find this one?

SALLY: I looked at doors until I came across it.

WOMAN: Then I should try the same again.

Eleven

SALLY: That's real rejection for you, Simon.

MAN: Find another doctor.

SALLY: I suppose so.

MAN: If you think something's wrong.

SALLY: I can't be bothered.

MAN: How do you feel?

SALLY: Fine but I think I can feel a lump.

MAN: Ask Mum what she thinks.

SALLY: She thinks it's the fibres in my bust sinking because I don't wear a bra.

MAN: They say you need up-lift.

SALLY: Who do?

MAN: Well –

SALLY: Come on, Simon, who do?

MAN: All the adverts you ever see for bras.

SALLY: I've been wearing mine solidly for the past two weeks, even in bed in case it made it go away. It doesn't make any difference.

MAN: Perhaps you haven't got the right sort.

SALLY: How come you're such an expert?

MAN: I read the bra ads.

SALLY: Do you read the ads or do you look at the bras?

MAN: What's in them, perhaps.

SALLY: I never think of you doing that, Si.

He said it was because I was frigid, that I wanted something wrong. An excuse. Women can have psychosomatic pregnancies.

MAN: More believable than breast lumps.

SALLY: But what if I have, Simon? What if it is cancer?

MAN: You have to be at least forty to get it.

SALLY: I read it can happen when you're younger.

MAN: Your chances must be pretty remote.

SALLY: How remote?

MAN: As winning the pools or something.

SALLY: People do win.

MAN: They aren't likely to be you.

SALLY: I suppose not.

Twelve

WOMAN: I must, I must, I must increase my bust.

SALLY: I must, I must, I must increase my bust.

WOMAN: I must, I must, I must increase my bust.

SALLY: It's a bit exhausting.

WOMAN: It's worth it.

SALLY: It had better be.

WOMAN: It really is.

SALLY: How many times do you have to do it?

WOMAN: Millions.

SALLY: We'll be worn out.

WOMAN: Don't you want to grow?

SALLY: Yes.

WOMAN: Then you have to do it. You have to do it a million times for every inch!

SALLY: One million?

WOMAN: Yes. But the results are amazing.

SALLY: That means if I want six inches I'll have to do six million!

WOMAN: I must, I must, I must increase my bust.

SALLY: I've only done about twenty.

WOMAN: It doesn't show until you've done half a million.

SALLY: Oh gosh.

WOMAN: And you mustn't lie on them in the night in between.

SALLY: Why not?

WOMAN: They get squashed in.

SALLY: Do they?

WOMAN: They get squashed right in.

SALLY: Then what happens?

WOMAN: I don't know.

SALLY: Don't they come out again?

WOMAN: No.

SALLY: How horrible.

WOMAN: They get ingrown like toenails.

SALLY: What do you do?

WOMAN: You have to put lots of pillows in your bed to sleep on.

SALLY: You can't do that.

WOMAN: Why?

SALLY: It makes your mouth come open when you're sleeping.

WOMAN: What difference does that make?

SALLY: It gives you double chins.

WOMAN: You've got them already.

SALLY: I haven't.

WOMAN: I've done nearly three thousand this week. Which means I'll get a bra first.

BOTH: I must, I must, I must increase my bust.

WOMAN: I can feel mine growing.

SALLY: Can you?

WOMAN: Yes.

SALLY: I can feel mine too.

Thirteen

WOMAN: Miss Bacon, Sally –

SALLY: I heard them calling me as I came back from the theatre –

WOMAN: Sally –

SALLY: I could hear them calling me as I floated back and made my way through thick grass –

WOMAN: Sally –

SALLY: Which swished as I walked and I felt that they couldn't see my head as I parted the green hay and scarlet poppies.

Oh Sally go and call the cattle home,
and call the cattle home,
and call the cattle home,
Across the sands of Dee:

The western wind was wild and dank with foam
And all alone went she.

I wouldn't open my eyes but I could hear them calling me.

WOMAN: Miss Bacon, Sally, Miss Bacon –

SALLY: Every morning here at seven, because they shake me to make me face the day –

WOMAN: Wakey, wakey, Miss Bacon –

SALLY: And do not allow me to slip back –

WOMAN: Open your eyes.

SALLY: Even to semi-fantasy –

WOMAN: That's a good girl –

SALLY: I see a shimmer of purple and green sea. I knew I was still alive and felt a moment of great elation. I wanted to stand on my bed in my white gown and shout, 'I am alive!' I will open my eyes.

WOMAN: They've had to take it.

SALLY: What – ?

WOMAN: They're sorry but they've had to take it off.

SALLY: No.

WOMAN: Shush. You're all right. It's gone to make you better. It was a malignant tumour.

SALLY: Have they got it all?

WOMAN: Yes.

SALLY: Is it all gone?

WOMAN: Yes.

SALLY: Have they got all of it? They haven't left any, have they?

WOMAN: No.

SALLY: I'm all right?

WOMAN: Right as rain. Would you like something to send you back to sleep?

SALLY: They said –

MAN: You will feel some discomfort. Perhaps a little aching and a sense of loss. But that will pass.

SALLY: Are you sure they've got it all?

WOMAN: Yes. That's why you can't feel anything. There's nothing there. That's it – you go back to sleep – that's it.

SALLY: I shut my eyes and there are no colours. No one has told me what they have done with it. Whether it collapsed itself to be accommodated, nipple upwards in one of those dishes, stainless steel and shaped like a kidney, or was it just put down somewhere, on some convenient surface after its nature of a pink blancmange with a cherry on top –

Sally no longer calls the cattle home,
calls the cattle home,
calls the cattle home,
Across the sands of Dee:
The western wind was wild and dank with
                                             foam
And all alone went she.

Fourteen

WOMAN: Yes?

SALLY: I've a lump.

WOMAN: Where?

SALLY: Here.

WOMAN: There?

SALLY: Yes. I've a lump.

MAN: Where?

SALLY: Here.

MAN: There?

SALLY: Yes. I've a lump.

WOMAN: Where?

SALLY: Here?

WOMAN: There?

SALLY: Yes. I've a lump.

MAN: Here?

SALLY: There!

WOMAN: Where?

SALLY: Here.

MAN: There?

SALLY: Where?

WOMAN: There?

SALLY: I've

BOTH: a lump –

MAN: Where?

WOMAN: There.

SALLY: Here!

Fifteen

SALLY: It's still there.

WOMAN: No it isn't, love. That's just the strapping and the bandages.

SALLY: Are you sure?

WOMAN: I promise you. You'll be able to have a look when we take the bandages off.

SALLY: I don't want to.

WOMAN: You'll have to look some time.

SALLY: I don't.

WOMAN: If you see it while it's really nasty you'll think it that much nicer when it heals.

SALLY: Is it horrid?

WOMAN: I expect it's a bit messy just at the moment.

SALLY: I never want to look at it.

WOMAN: You will – in time.

I find it hard to nurse these women, who remind me of my mother and my sisters. And wonder how I would feel lying there. For all I feel pity and sorrow but with these women I feel guilty – and wonder if it will ever be me.

Sixteen

MAN: I'm worried for Sally, my daughter. I want to help.

Sally, if there's anything –

SALLY: My father had found a time for us to be alone.

MAN: Anything.

SALLY: And I notice that my father is growing old.

MAN: Tell me.

SALLY: And I think perhaps I have always been close to this man who turns his coins over in his pockets.

MAN: Do you want it done privately?

SALLY: I was uneasy when my father said –

MAN: I can pay for you.

SALLY: I said 'Dad' and let him continue.

MAN: We can afford it. Would you feel better if I did that?

SALLY: The subject is so awkward I can say nothing about it.

MAN: You'd get it done at once.

SALLY: They do it as quickly as they can.

MAN: Can you be sure?

SALLY: They do, Dad.

MAN: I suppose so. You'd get good nursing.

SALLY: It's okay, Dad.

MAN: And the privacy. You might want to be private.

SALLY: Yes.

MAN: There are advantages.

SALLY: I know. Matching cups and saucers and lunch in bed and not being woken in the morning and being able to have coffee at tea time and being able to sleep with flowers in my room at night.

MAN: It's the treatment you get.

SALLY: The surgeon you had used to operate at the General in the mornings.

MAN: Let me help.

SALLY: They're expecting me at the General.

MAN: I could change it.

SALLY: No, Dad. I need to be with other women.

Pause.

I didn't want Simon to tell you. A cyst isn't serious, Dad.

MAN: Are they sure it's a cyst?

Pause.

SALLY: No.

MAN: Life isn't fair.

SALLY: No.

MAN: I look at this strange woman who sits with her eyes on the road. It is dark. I watch my daughter who will not look but stares at the road and knows I am watching her.

SALLY: I rang my father late in the evening.

MAN: I found my daughter that night. With her flat door shut behind her and her keys in her bag. She put her case in the boot and sat in the car. We did not touch each other and she said –

SALLY: Will Mum make me cocoa?

WOMAN: On paper Sally's breasts are minutely complicated. Their components interlaced like a clump of trees on the skyline before the dawn. Blue, blues and bluish. The first mammogram I saw I was astonished that women are like that inside.

SALLY: I look at the dark.

WOMAN: In one there is a blue shadow like the moon behind thick clouds.

Seventeen

SALLY: Oh Zoey –

WOMAN: I am a friend. Because I am a friend I went to Sainsbury's to buy fruit. I was going to buy chocolate, but if I, Zoey am expected to share, I had rather be indulged in grapes. I wanted to bring black ones or the tiny seedless ones. I notice some have fallen off the stem and crushed. Always select.

I'm sorry.

SALLY: I wouldn't recognise it.

WOMAN: What?

SALLY: My boob. I wouldn't know that it was mine. I wouldn't.

WOMAN: Have a good cry about it. Afterwards you'll feel better.

SALLY: Why do people keep telling me that I'll feel better after crying?

WOMAN: You always do.

SALLY: I've cried a lot. And every time I dry my eyes I think – that's it. All over. It isn't.

WOMAN: Look, you have a cry about it.

SALLY: This woman, though not my closest or most amusing, is my oldest friend. She is the most flat-chested.

Eighteen

SALLY: What are you doing?

WOMAN: What's it look like?

SALLY: I don't know.

WOMAN: Bet you do.

SALLY: They're your socks. Why are you putting knots in your socks?

WOMAN: I'm making nipples.

SALLY: Are you?

WOMAN: When I get them knotted right.

SALLY: Really?

WOMAN: See.

SALLY: They're too big!

WOMAN: How do you know?

SALLY: Nobody has nipples like that!

WOMAN: Ladies with real bosoms do.

SALLY: They don't.

WOMAN: How do you know?

SALLY: My Mum doesn't.

WOMAN: Have you see your Mum's?

SALLY: Yes.

WOMAN: When?

SALLY: Sometimes.

WOMAN: How many times?

SALLY: Often.

WOMAN: Is often more times than lots?

SALLY: Lots. Her's aren't like that.

WOMAN: That's because your mother hasn't got proper ones.

SALLY: Zoey was the only one who had the style to venture out with nipples. I have never seen my mother's breasts.

Nineteen

MAN: Next please. Yes?

SALLY: I've got a lump. In my breast.

MAN: Are you pre-menstrual?

SALLY: No.

MAN: Any pain?

SALLY: No. Why?

MAN: Pain usually means it's mastitis.

SALLY: Will you examine me?

MAN: Of course. Just slip your top things off.

Which breast?

SALLY: My left one.

MAN: Where?

SALLY: Here.

MAN: There.

SALLY: Can you feel it? That's where it is.

MAN: I see.

SALLY: It's not the same as the other one, is it?

MAN: No. I'm afraid I don't think it is.

SALLY: It's a lump?

MAN: There is something there.

SALLY: Oh God!

MAN: Most probably a cyst.

SALLY: That's what everybody says.

MAN: Everybody?

SALLY: People – when I tell them I've got a lump.

MAN: Why tell them and not seek proper medical advice?

SALLY: I have. But no one's taken me seriously. Now I'm frightened.

MAN: You are, aren't you.

SALLY: Wouldn't you be?

MAN: In your position? Yes, I think I'd be terrified. How long's it been troubling you?

SALLY: I'm not sure.

MAN: You must have some idea?

SALLY: I first thought I found it about four months ago.

MAN: Has it increased in size since then?

SALLY: I don't know. I didn't think it had.

MAN: Wishful thinking?

SALLY: Everybody said it was mastitis or nothing. That I was going through a bad time and imagining it.

MAN: And you took their word for it?

SALLY: I thought they'd find it at the FPA.

MAN: I might not have found it if you hadn't pinpointed it so accurately.

SALLY: Then am I right?

MAN: Let's let the dog see the rabbit.

SALLY: What?

MAN: Shine a bright light through it. Anything hollow, like a fluid filled cyst will show up as a shadow and we'll be able to aspirate it.

I'm afraid it looks pretty solid.

SALLY: More serious?

MAN: Not necessarily. We'll just have to look further into it.

SALLY: Operate on it?

MAN: My jokes aren't that bad. We might, as a very last resort, we might have to biopsy it.

SALLY: Biopsy?

MAN: We remove a bit of tissue for examination. But that's unlikely. I'll send you up to outpatients for a mammogram.

SALLY: A what?

MAN: It's a technique of x-raying the breast, only the print appears on paper and not on film.

SALLY: What's it called?

MAN: The technique? A mammogram. Don't worry, it's perfectly painless. I'll get an appointment made as soon as possible.

SALLY: Thank you.

Twenty

SALLY: I have a scene where a lover comes to me in tears and buries his face between my breasts and cries.

MAN: I am an ex-lover. Because I am an ex-lover and therefore no longer care about her putting on weight and having to secure her jeans with safety pins, I have brought her chocolates. Because I am an ex-lover and not quite a friend, I have bought a box without a ribbon, not soft centres. Choosing in a shop which graded its goodies towards the ceiling and in a state of financial cut back, I chose the level just above the jelly fruits.

She looks ghastly and I ask her if she is OK.

SALLY: Because he is my ex-lover I am embarrassed by him being here. His seeing me like this. I tell him I am fine, remember to smile and ask him how he is.

MAN: I tell her that I'm well and that she's looking good.

SALLY: I tell him I'm feeling better than I thought I would and isn't it a lovely day?

MAN: I tell her it's colder than it looks and that I'm sorry I didn't bring her flowers.

SALLY: I tell him it's a bad time of the year for cut flowers but chocolates, he shouldn't have, how lovely.

MAN: I tell her it's a pleasure.

SALLY: I tell him I'll get fat.

MAN: I tell her I expect the food here is dreadful.

SALLY: I tell him it isn't that bad.

MAN: I tell her that –

SALLY: I tell him that –

MAN: I tell her –

SALLY: I tell him –

MAN: I tell –

SALLY: I tell –

MAN: I –

SALLY: I –

MAN: I kiss her goodbye when I leave and say nothing about coming again. There are no promises made about seeing each other and I don't know why I came unless it was to see I left a box of chocolates by her bed. I wonder what will become of her.

SALLY: For the first time, I look.

Twenty-one

MAN: Bags I be doctor.

WOMAN: I'm the nurse.

MAN: You're the patient.

SALLY: Why?

MAN: Because I'm the doctor and she's the nurse so you've got to be.

SALLY: I don't want to be.

WOMAN: You didn't bags.

SALLY: I didn't know we had to.

WOMAN: That's your fault. I've got to be a nurse because I've got a nurse's uniform.

SALLY: Can we bags again?

MAN: No.

SALLY: Let's do something different.

MAN: We're doing this. I'm going to do an operation.

SALLY: No.

WOMAN: Are you going to cut her open, doctor?

MAN: Yes.

WOMAN: Then she's got to take her vest off.

SALLY: Leave me alone.

WOMAN: Doctors have to look.

SALLY: For the first time, I look.

MAN: I'm going to cut you open and take all the badness out of you.

SALLY: It's still there!

WOMAN: No love, it's just the strappings and the bandages.

Twenty-two

MAN: Hello, Sliced Bacon.

WOMAN: Simon!

SALLY: It's okay, Mum.

WOMAN: How are you, darling?

SALLY: I'm fine.

MAN: Shall I leave you and come back?

SALLY: Stay.

WOMAN: Please. I've brought you this and these and I thought you'd like this and these and Simon's got this for you.

SALLY: Mum, you shouldn't have.

WOMAN: Is that everything, Simon?

MAN: I think so.

WOMAN: We forgot the flowers.

SALLY: It doesn't matter, Mum.

MAN: I could go back for them.

SALLY: There's no need. Bring me them tomorrow.

WOMAN: Is there anything else you need?

SALLY: Nothing.

WOMAN: I wish you could come home.

SALLY: So do I, Mum. I want to sit in the garden and talk.

Twenty-three

SALLY: Fleur, they won't believe me.

WOMAN: You'll have to go back again, Sal.

SALLY: Again? I do nothing but, and still nobody does anything.

WOMAN: They can't stop you going back as many times as you want.

SALLY: It's getting to the stage when I think I daren't show my face again.

WOMAN: Sally, it's your body, you've got to take yourself seriously.

SALLY: I do but they won't. Officially this time it's nerves. I've got the tranquillisers to prove it.

WOMAN: You taking them?

SALLY: No.

WOMAN: It's the same old story. Give her something, she'll be OK. Look at the way they fobbed me off with my cyst. Have you had a physical examination?

SALLY: No. That's what I can't understand, I go in and they ask me what's wrong and I tell them and they write out another prescription. The last one told me I was imagining it. Four months, imagining!

WOMAN: Has it got bigger since the last time you checked?

SALLY: I daren't check. I can't bring myself to.

WOMAN: Come on, it's every month. Every single month.

SALLY: Do you check every month?

WOMAN: Listen Sal, it's probably nothing serious – most breast lumps are benign, but you've got to make certain.

SALLY: I'm scared, Fleur.

WOMAN: I know. I dread checking. Every month I think 'What if I find another?' I do it when everyone else is out. I always have to look in the mirror first, just in case there's something obvious like puckering or the nipple inverting. I'm so nervous and my fingers are tense. I have to make myself touch them. It's like that every month, Sal. It has to be. Those moments of being frightened of your own body. Do you know how to check?

SALLY: Yes. Like this.

WOMAN: No, you must do it properly. That way you're going to pick up all the natural masses in the breast. Watch, it's like this, with your hand flat and the fingers gently together. In the bath with soap on your hands is much the best time. That way your hand just glides over the breast and the fingers will pick up any lumps that are there. Like this. Two sweeps then down and part the fingers as you pass the hand over the nipple.

SALLY: It's so awkward.

WOMAN: No, it's simple and it's quick. How could you forget to do something so easy?

I should have offered to check my friend's breasts.

Twenty-four

SALLY: Suddenly I am certain.

WOMAN: Name?

SALLY: Sally Bacon.

WOMAN: Forenames?

SALLY: Sally Deborah.

WOMAN: Age?

SALLY: Twenty-nine.

WOMAN: Religion?

SALLY: None.

WOMAN: Next of kin?

SALLY: Simon Bacon.

WOMAN: Relationship?

SALLY: Brother.

Twenty-five

MAN: Because she has asked me to, I am the one who copes. Sally is my responsibility. I am the one who goes to the hospital and waits like an expectant father.

WOMAN: Mr Bacon?

MAN: Yes?

WOMAN: You're Miss Bacon's brother?

MAN: Yes, is she all right?

WOMAN: I'm sorry, it was malignant. We've had to take the breast.

MAN: That's what she was frightened of. Losing it.

WOMAN: What's important is that we've caught the cancer.

MAN: Can I see her? I want to tell her.

WOMAN: It's best that we tell her. You come this evening.

MAN: Yes.

WOMAN: Help her get back to normal.

MAN: Normal. What is normal after losing a breast? I don't know. What is it like without a breast? What does it feel like? How does she feel? Is it a loss or a change? Is she different? Is there a difference?

Twenty-six

WOMAN: OK?

SALLY: I just sign it?

WOMAN: You just sign your normal signature there and that gives us your permission to do the operation.

SALLY: I sign.

Twenty-seven

MAN: 'Scuse me love, can I fix the headset?

SALLY: What?

MAN: Headset?

SALLY: Oh, yes.

MAN: You're looking lovely this morning. Gorgeous day.

SALLY: Yes.

MAN: What you in for?

SALLY: Check up.

MAN: Days in bed, nice and cosy. Perhaps I ought to get checked.

SALLY: What's wrong with it?

MAN: Got pulled out the wall. Got brute strength some of them in here.

SALLY: Yes.

MAN: You weren't the one? Pulled it out?

SALLY: I've only been in four days.

MAN: Teasing you, love. Know the sort of pulling you do with a body like yours. I like voluptuous women.

SALLY: Me. Why me? Me. Why me? Why me? Why me? Why me?

Twenty-eight

SALLY: My TB test?

MAN: You banged your breast.

SALLY: From too much sport?

WOMAN: Lack of support.

SALLY: From being caressed?

MAN: You're overstressed.

SALLY: Some childhood ill?

WOMAN: You're on the pill.

SALLY: From over eating?

MAN: Hormone secreting.

SALLY: Some unknown pest?

WOMAN: Bra wearing's best.

SALLY: From carrying bags?

MAN: From smoking fags?

SALLY: The drugs I've had?

WOMAN: From being bad.

Twenty-nine

MAN: Peep, peep, peep.
    You're getting bosoms!

SALLY: I'm not!

MAN: You are. Girls always do.

SALLY: I'm not.

MAN: Don't you want to have bosoms?

SALLY: No!

MAN: I thought girls wanted to?

SALLY: I don't.

MAN: But you will.

SALLY: I won't.

MAN: How do you know?

SALLY: I just won't.

MAN: Bet you do.

SALLY: Bet I don't.

MAN: Go on then, bet.

MAN: When you get bosoms, you'll get like Mum.

SALLY: Will I?

    Peep, peep, peep, peep.

Thirty

MAN: Hello?

SALLY: Hello?

MAN: Sally?

SALLY: Simon?

MAN: Yes?

SALLY: It's me.

MAN: Sally? Is something wrong?

SALLY: Something's terrible.

MAN: OK, OK, I'm listening.

SALLY: I've got something wrong. I've got a lump in my breast – and so it could be –

MAN: Peep, peep, peep, peep.
    What?

SALLY: Cancer.

MAN: Crabs?

SALLY: Cancer, Simon. Don't tell mother.

MAN: Why?

SALLY: Don't.

MAN: It's not a secret I can store up about my sister.

Thirty-one

WOMAN: 'Morning, Simon.

MAN: 'Morning, Mum.

WOMAN: Was that Sally ringing last night?

MAN: Why?

WOMAN: She always rings so late to talk to you.

MAN: Yes.

WOMAN: Well, what did she say?

MAN: Nothing.

WOMAN: You were on the 'phone for hours.

MAN: She didn't say anything.

WOMAN: Is she well?

MAN: She's got a lump – they've found a lump. In her breast.

WOMAN: Sally's?

MAN: Yes.

WOMAN: Oh Simon –

MAN: I was silly about it. Mum, I just couldn't think what to say.

WOMAN: She said she thought she felt something – I thought – you know. You never know what's supposed to be there or not. You just don't know.

MAN: She said it's probably nothing.

WOMAN: What's going to happen?

MAN: She's got to go into hospital for a biopsy. Mum, she didn't want me to tell you. She's going to write you and Dad a letter.

WOMAN: I want to know.

MAN: So I tell my mother and she tells my father and we don't talk about it at supper that night.

Why Sally?

SALLY: Why me?

WOMAN: Why my daughter?

SALLY: I am not aware of being happy, or content or unhappy. Why me?

WOMAN: As Sally's mother I watched her changing and becoming a woman. Her body taking on contours.

Thirty-two

WOMAN: Why Sally?

SALLY: Why can't I have a bra?

WOMAN: You don't need one.

SALLY: Everybody else has got them.

WOMAN: But you haven't got anything to put in it.

SALLY: I have.

WOMAN: I didn't have a bra until I was sixteen.

SALLY: Mum, please. All my friends have got them.

WOMAN: All your friends?

SALLY: Lots of them.

WOMAN: I suppose Zoey has?

SALLY: Yes.

WOMAN: Zoey's chest is practically a hollow.

SALLY: So if she's got one I ought to have.

WOMAN: You don't have to have everything Zoey has.

SALLY: Please, Mum.

WOMAN: You've got vests.

SALLY: Vests aren't grown up.

WOMAN: I wear a vest.

SALLY: You have a bra under it. I flop about. Look, see! See me flopping!

WOMAN: You haven't got anything to flop.

SALLY: Yes, I have. Flop, flop.

WOMAN: The only thing that's flopping is your jumper because you've pulled it off by the sleeves and stretched it.

SALLY: Mum, I've got to have one.

WOMAN: Why?

SALLY: I've got nipples.

WOMAN: Ladies are born with those.

SALLY: But Zoey says that you've got to cover them up.

WOMAN: Zoey talks a lot of rubbish.

SALLY: But you've got to have uplift. It says on the packets that they give uplift. Zoey says that if you don't have uplift they just grow until they reach the floor.

WOMAN: I'm not buying you a bra until you need one.

SALLY: Then I'll ask Dad to buy me one.

WOMAN: Sally, you don't talk to men about things like that. Not if you're old enough to have a bra.

SALLY: Will you buy me one then.

WOMAN: You won't like it.

SALLY: 'Cos if you do, Mum, then I won't have to ask Dad, will I?

WOMAN: OK, you win.

SALLY: You've promised. Do you think it will make me look nice?

Thirty-three

SALLY: I think I will never again feel good because of it. Because if any one says –

MAN: You look good.

SALLY: I will think of this scar, curling across me. Buried in my skin. The vivid crest of the knife gash and the speckling of stitches. When I look in the mirror and think I am looking thinner it will always be right shoulder to the mirror.

Then I will turn full frontal and see one breast approaching opulence, I will always notice it curving round me and marking 'It was here'. I am disgusted. My mark of degradation. It is so humiliating and demanding of attention. I can't think that if I forget it – the fear will go away.

Thirty-four

SALLY: Simon, would you sleep with a woman without a breast?

MAN: I suppose so.

SALLY: How do you mean, I suppose?

MAN: I suppose I could.

SALLY: You could bring yourself to.

MAN: It's not a question of bringing yourself to.

SALLY: So you could?

MAN: I would if she turned me on.

SALLY: Would she still turn you on?

MAN: If we'd got that far I don't suppose it would turn me off.

SALLY: Would it be the same?

MAN: I don't know.

SALLY: Think!

MAN: I don't suppose it would be different.

SALLY: It wouldn't be the same?

MAN: It's never the same.

SALLY: Don't you think? If she only had one?

MAN: That's not what it's all about.

SALLY: Isn't it?

MAN: It's about people not breasts.

SALLY: But if it came to it?

MAN: It's not the sort of thing you think about.

SALLY: Never?

MAN: I've never thought about it.

SALLY: I have. Often. Of loving men who have been mutilated. Because they were. Women can love men who are wrecks, it's traditional.

MAN: Women can be loved too.

SALLY: Can a lover bury his face between a lone breast?

Thirty-five

WOMAN: Mastectomy, isn't it?

Can tell by the way you use your arm.

SALLY: It's sore.

WOMAN: Will be for a bit. Mine was.

SALLY: Have you had it done?

WOMAN: Twice. It spread. I've got secondaries. Makes you wonder why they do it if they don't stop it. They said if nothing happened for five years they thought I'd be OK. Four and a half years I'd gone.

SALLY: I'm sorry.

WOMAN: Didn't think it could happen. Not after everything else. I thought if anything else happened I'd go out of my mind. I haven't, I go on. He went after the first one. Thought he'd caused it at first, being a bit rough with me there. But they say it didn't. Couldn't have the second time. Our marriage wasn't much good before, just worse after. Wonder who'll want me with none?

SALLY: No one will be able to tell.

WOMAN: I've got four boys, they'll think we're a scout group. They did a radical the first time. Cut from here to here. They said it was a shame they didn't find it earlier. I wasn't to know, was I? I did this time though. This one's a simple. It is neater.

SALLY: Mine's a simple. They call it a simple.

WOMAN: It might be for them. It isn't for us. Not if you have to explain it – especially to the kids. First time I told them it had gone to make Mummy better. What am I going to tell them this time? It must have happened for a reason. Least that's what I keep telling myself. But I can't see one. Can you?

SALLY: It just happens.

WOMAN: I could understand it if there was a reason. I could try.

SALLY: You have to be brave.

WOMAN: What's being brave? You have it, what else can you do? I don't want to die, I'm not frightened of it now but I don't want to. Not until the children – you see that's what frightens me. What happens to them. For them it's not how you look, is it? It's being there. That's all I want. Didn't have time to worry, not until

I got here. Just rushing round trying to get everything ready. All I wanted was just to get here, get it done, get out and get back to looking after them. I'm so tired that I think I can't go on. You do. You get so strong. And if you're busy you don't have time to think.

SALLY: I touch myself in search of cancer for two minutes out of the thirty-five thousand, four hundred and twenty there are in each month of the moon. I spend five minutes a day making sure I cross roads properly. More women die of cancer of the breast when it spreads into secondaries than are killed every year on the road. More women than all the people I will ever meet.

Thirty-six

MAN: Sal, can I see your tits?

SALLY: Simon, they're bosoms.

MAN: Why aren't they tits?

SALLY: Tits is crude.

MAN: Who says tits is crude?

SALLY: Mum does.

MAN: You mean rude!

SALLY: Crude is nastier than rude.

MAN: What's the difference?

SALLY: Ask Mum.

MAN: Can I see your bosoms, then?

SALLY: No.

MAN: But I want to see some real ones.

SALLY: Why?

MAN: I just do.

SALLY: They're just the same.

MAN: They aren't.

SALLY: How do you know if you haven't seen any?

MAN: We found this magazine in the park. It was all torn up and we had to find all the bits and it was full of ladies with no clothes on. And I said I'd ask you if I could see yours because I'm the only one who's got a sister. And if you show them to Terry King he'll give me his United scarf. Will you, Sally?

SALLY: No.

MAN: Why not?

SALLY: It's not nice!

MAN: These ladies haven't got any clothes on.

SALLY: None at all?

MAN: Here. I'm sorry they're all torn up.

SALLY: I don't look like that!

MAN: I didn't think you did. I told them you didn't.

SALLY: That wasn't fair.

MAN: Well you don't.

SALLY: I'm still developing.

MAN: I don't think she looks very nice.

SALLY: No, they don't look real.

MAN: Do you think you'll develop as big as that?

SALLY: I don't know. You can't tell.

Thirty-seven

SALLY: Afterwards they said –

MAN: You will feel some aching and a sense of loss.

SALLY: I do not go out and buy myself dresses or pamper myself in the bath because I am ashamed. I think of the hospital as warm and safe and the place where I was comforted.

You can't tell?

WOMAN: No and that's only a temporary prosthesis to protect the wound.

SALLY: I know the second I lay my hand about it I will cry.

Hold me tightly, please. Hold me tightly. Hold me.

WOMAN: Is that tight enough.

SALLY: Tighter, please, tighter.

I cry between two warm breasts and wish they were those of my mother. I'm so alone.

WOMAN: Not here. There's me. The nurses, the doctors, everyone else here, all your family and your friends. There are so many women who come here more alone than you and who are twice as lonely when they leave. There are some women here who make a fuss, because here at least they know the fuss will be listened to. Those aren't lonely women, they are isolated.

SALLY: I want to go home.

WOMAN: Of course you do. But we can't discharge you until you're ready. You'll feel better, you know. Once you're dressed. More like the real you.

SALLY: Yes.

Who does she mean by that? I want to be held until the fingers bruise the skin on my arm until I shake with being held and holding.

Thirty-eight

SALLY: Don't!

MAN: Come on.

SALLY: Don't!

MAN: Come on.

God – you're tense.

SALLY: Don't touch me! Please.

MAN: I'm sorry.

SALLY: You mustn't touch me.

MAN: OK, Sal.

SALLY: I'm sorry.

MAN: It's OK.

SALLY: I have prepared speeches for this moment. It's false.

MAN: Let me.

SALLY: No.

MAN: Kiss me.

SALLY: I have a lover.

Thirty-nine

WOMAN: Did sister give you your outpatients card?

SALLY: Yes.

I can't carry this.

MAN: I'll take it.

SALLY: When I stand up my father holds my coat open for me. I fumble with the buttons and the nurse has already stripped the bed and I learn that all mattresses are disinfected, not only those of the dead.

WOMAN: Goodbye. Take care.

SALLY: Neither she nor I know whether or not we are supposed to shake hands and I can't remember if there is a protocol. From hospital drama slots I have a notion that now the closing credits should come up on the screen as we walk towards the entrance of the ward and do not look back.

MAN: Should I have brought them something?

SALLY: Why, Dad?

MAN: You know, a little present. Just to say thank you.

SALLY: There are so many.

MAN: Yes.

SALLY: They've been very good to me.

MAN: Come on. The car's just round the corner.

SALLY: I can't, Dad.

MAN: Sally?

SALLY: I can't go out there.

MAN: Yes, you can. Just round the corner down the steps.

SALLY: They'll look at me.

MAN: They won't.

SALLY: They will. They'll all be looking.

MAN: I thought you wanted to get out.

SALLY: They'll all know.

MAN: They won't.

SALLY: Everybody's staring at me.

MAN: Why should they be looking at you?

SALLY: They will.

MAN: You've got to get used to it. Your mother's waiting.

SALLY: Can I take your arm? I have learnt to be dependent.

Bosom implies the corporate identity of the mammary glands. Corresponding nerves, blood vessels et al. Two.

Forty

WOMAN: I am a mother expecting her daughter home.

SALLY: I am a daughter arriving home.

WOMAN: Sally, darling!

SALLY: Hello, Mum.

WOMAN: On the outside there is no sign, I wonder if my daughter has lost her chances.

Did you have a good journey?

SALLY: Fine, thanks.

WOMAN: I've aired your bed. Do you want to get in?

SALLY: No.

WOMAN: A little rest?

SALLY: I'm not ill!

WOMAN: I know. But half an hour with your feet up? You needn't get in.

SALLY: She pulls back the bedspread, indicating it must be half an hour with my feet up, between the sheets. I have come home because they care.

WOMAN: I am glad to have my daughter home.

SALLY: She puts my underwear away and does not comment on it, although she is not familiar with it as she was when I lived at home and she did my washing and I liked her to. She puts things in exactly the same places in the drawers as she did when I was younger. It is the same system as my grandmother's. It has been passed down amongst the women of the family. She sits on my bed as she did when I was a child and slept with the door open and the light on in the night.

WOMAN: My mother said her mother died of a wasting disease.

SALLY: Was it cancer?

WOMAN: I don't know. We didn't talk about it. Are the risks of having it in your breast higher if it runs in the family? In the mother's line?

SALLY: They don't say so.

WOMAN: Is it because of me? Something in me. Is it my fault? Tell me.

SALLY: Even if it were known I could not acknowledge the blame on this woman.

WOMAN: It's too close for comfort.

SALLY: Do you check?

WOMAN: I never have.

SALLY: Not checking doesn't mean you never get it.

WOMAN: Do it for me.

SALLY: I place my skin on the flesh from which it came and can feel her heart beating under my pulse.

In the night it is worst. Sometimes in the night I can't go to sleep in case I am dead when I wake up. I am more afraid of that than I am of being followed at night on a dark street. I do not want to be a victim without a struggle.

Forty-one

MAN: Do you want sympathy?

SALLY: My boss makes me coffee and offers me a biscuit.

MAN: My wife doesn't eat to compensate. She can't.

SALLY: He says.

MAN: My wife's arms are useless. They didn't catch hers in time. She doesn't have any breasts. After they treated her with chemotherapy she lost her hair.

SALLY: I have never seen his wife. I know she is a cripple and many times we have discussed between ourselves behind his back whether he is still faithful.

MAN: You are one of the lucky ones. What have you really lost?

SALLY: He offers me a biscuit and I refuse.

MAN: Nothing. It's in her bones. She is waiting for the cancer to creep over her and through her until she can't resist it. Until she becomes it. My wife will die of cancer slowly.

SALLY: The place which is empty aches.

MAN: I have to dress my wife in the morning. I have to undress her at night. Soon I won't be able to and someone else will have to manage, and someone else after that until her body becomes universal.

SALLY: I am a breast and a lymph node lighter.

MAN: It is the thoughts that weigh you down, whether she thought because I had admired her body that I meant it must be complete. She says there is no one to blame. But if there is no blame I cannot understand the unfairness of it. She says she is happy and has been happy and I wonder if that is because she is unhappy now. Her life has not been big or exciting but she says she is fulfilled. I cannot bear to see her pulled apart. People are sympathetic. It is my isolation from hope that is drowning me. She wrecked her life trying to keep her body whole. I did not ask her to be beautiful but to be there.

SALLY: The sun is warm on my thigh.

MAN: We sit together in silence and stillness.

SALLY: A lover.

Forty-two

SALLY: Outpatients?

MAN: Gate 1.

WOMAN: Wait.

MAN: Block 2.

WOMAN: Wait.

MAN: Floor 4.

WOMAN: Wait.

MAN: Room 5.

WOMAN: Wait. Room change.

MAN: Room 6.

WOMAN: Patient?

MAN: Miss Bacon.

Forty-three

SALLY: I went into hospital to have a lump taken out of my breast. I woke up and the breast was gone. They'd cut it off. So I knew I had cancer.

WOMAN: And did they prepare you for the possibility of losing your breast?

SALLY: They told me I might.

WOMAN: And did they make it clear that you have a choice to be woken up after the biopsy. You have a legal right to know that the lump is malignant before they take the breast.

SALLY: What difference does that make?

WOMAN: It can make the waking less traumatic. You ought to see about getting a proper prosthesis. It needs to be weighted so you don't pull round to compensate. It's a lovely scar.

SALLY: Do you think so?

WOMAN: It's not going to stop you wearing a low-cut dress or bikini or anything.

SALLY: Going without a bra?

WOMAN: I don't see why you shouldn't have a breast implant done in the future.

SALLY: Sorry?

WOMAN: They insert a pad of silicone under the skin so you have a reshaped breast. They can't give you a life-like nipple yet but breast surgery techniques are improving all the time. Who knows.

SALLY: I could have it done?

WOMAN: I don't see why not. Unlike a prosthesis it will last you for life.

SALLY: How long's that going to be?

WOMAN: Your prognosis is good.

SALLY: Five years – ten – or am I completely cured?

WOMAN: We don't know yet. We haven't found an answer.

SALLY: The doctor goes to wash her hands.

WOMAN: Cancer is a cell run riot. An anarchist in the body. Cancer is the self-motivated, self-supporting growth of tissue.

SALLY: She washes her hands.

WOMAN: It starts from one single, malignant, mutant cell.

SALLY: She has washed her hands.

WOMAN: With cancer you never know if the war is over, or if it is just a long ceasefire.

SALLY: Cancer is.

Forty-four

SALLY: I don't want to be a victim without a struggle.

Help me! Help me! Help me! Hear! Hear! Hear!

MAN: Sally?

SALLY: Hear!

MAN: Wake up, wake up, Sally. It's only a dream.

SALLY: I'm sorry.

MAN: It's OK.

SALLY: I was running. But I was running after something and away from something else.

MAN: It's OK.

SALLY: Could you tell when you looked at me?

MAN: What?

SALLY: That I didn't have it.

MAN: I thought you did.

SALLY: Did you?

MAN: Of course I did. You expect women to.

SALLY: So you just thought I did?

MAN: Why should I have thought anything else?

SALLY: Because it shows.

MAN: You can't tell.

SALLY: It bulges at the side.

MAN: When I told my dad he said 'That's amazing'. It looks better than the real thing. Which one is it, anyway?

SALLY: Did he?

MAN: He couldn't tell. I could have taken money on it.

SALLY: Why did you tell him?

MAN: So he could get my mother to check.

SALLY: Did she?

MAN: I think so.

SALLY: I'll ring her in the morning and make sure.

MAN: You didn't mind me telling him?

SALLY: I don't suppose so – no.

MAN: So you needn't worry about it.

SALLY: What do you mean?

MAN: If he knows, what matter who else does?

SALLY: You beast.

MAN: I love you.

SALLY: Do you?

MAN: The Amazons were very sexy women. Hence their power. Their captives just swooned and fell at their feet. It was a walk-over.

SALLY: You make me laugh.

MAN: That's the sort of woman to get hold of, said my father. A woman who gets all her bras half-price. You'll be able to drink champagne on that.

Forty-five

MAN: Nice to see you.

WOMAN: Feeling better?

MAN: Are you well.

WOMAN: Glad you're back.

MAN: How you feeling?

WOMAN: We have missed you.

MAN: Where have you been?

WOMAN: How do you feel?

MAN: Thought you'd left.

WOMAN: Were you ill?

MAN: You're looking good.

WOMAN: What have they done?

SALLY: I realise that they are pleased to see me and that though I have told my boss he has respected me and not told them what has been done. I notice the cloakroom pegs are rearranged and a bottom one left empty for me.

Forty-six

SALLY: Suddenly I find I am standing naked in front of a mirror, watching the movements I can make with my body. And I notice that the marking I thought was livid and red is pale and tired and has sunk into the skin and that though there is no breast, there is no hole on me on the skin which is smooth and moves mysteriously. And I think it is fine and fun to stand in front of this mirror and to feel the air on my skin, I wonder what it would be like in a breeze. And in the mirror I touch myself.

MAN: She undresses for me for the first time. But does not turn out the light as I thought she would. Do I look or do I turn away? I am so frightened of being awkward about it. And if I look, should I say, and if I say will she take it the wrong way? I don't want to turn away from her. She takes off her jumper pulling on the sleeves, a butterfly struggling out of its cocoon. Her bra. For a second she pauses, intent on herself. I look at this woman and her body and it is sensuous.

Forty-seven

WOMAN: All this fuss about a pound of flesh.

MAN: God moves in mysterious ways.

WOMAN: It's not as if you're married.

MAN: It's only a bit of tissue.

SALLY: I watch myself.

Forty-eight

WOMAN: Sally!

SALLY: Fleur.

WOMAN: What are you doing?

SALLY: I've cleaned them twice this week. It's supposed to be good exercise for the muscles in my arm. They wrenched them when they clamped my arm back for the operation.

WOMAN: Sally, there's something – I have to say it.

SALLY: It's OK, Fleur.

WOMAN: When Simon rang me and said you'd had it done I thought – thank God it hasn't happened to me. Like that.

SALLY: I know.

WOMAN: I was so relieved. I even went to the hospital, not to see you but to get mine checked –

SALLY: They didn't find anything?

WOMAN: No, nothing there. Thank God. I'm sorry, Sal.

SALLY: I missed you.

WOMAN: Did you want me to come?

SALLY: Yes. When you didn't I guessed it was because it brought back memories of your cyst.

WOMAN: You came to see me.

SALLY: So what?

WOMAN: I wanted to see you and yet I couldn't come.

SALLY: You've come now.

WOMAN: But it doesn't make up for it.

SALLY: I'd have felt the same way. When I came to see you I didn't look at you once. Just trying to see if I could see where they'd done it. You had a horrid nightie.

WOMAN: Thanks.

SALLY: That's one thing I've got out of it, nighties. I had one when I first went in. I had five coming out. All the relatives sent me them.

WOMAN: You do look well.

SALLY: Roses in my cheeks and everything?

WOMAN: How do you feel?

SALLY: Like a woman without a breast, numb. They're being wonderful here. Mum's doing a great job, being practical and strict and encouraging and jollying me along. Well, you know Mum. Dad's more discreet about it. He's moved the bathroom mirror so I can't see myself in the bath any more. The funny thing is that the more careful they are – the more I know I'm being protected.

WOMAN: You can't be all the time.

SALLY: That's why it doesn't protect me at all. I can't see myself in the bath but everywhere there are whole women staring at me.

WOMAN: You're a whole woman.

SALLY: They're symmetrical women, Fleur, I'm not and I'm never going to be.

WOMAN: Come on, I'm taking you out for lunch.

SALLY: Fleur, I can't.

WOMAN: Who else is taking you?

SALLY: No one.

WOMAN: So you can.

SALLY: I can't go out. I can't.

WOMAN: Who's to know? I know you've had it done and I can't tell. The only clue I've got is the way you're cleaning windows and we aren't going window cleaning.

SALLY: I don't want to.

WOMAN: Of course you do. Pizza and ice cream?

SALLY: That's bribery.

WOMAN: Yes.

SALLY: No.

WOMAN: Sally, if you don't pull yourself together now it's going to be too late. The longer you put it off the worse it's going to get. OK, so there are people out there. Millions of them, and thousands of those are women without breasts. What makes you exceptional?

SALLY: They look at me.

WOMAN: So they don't bump into you, Sally. Come on.

Forty-nine

SALLY: Can I have children?

MAN: We do advise against it.

SALLY: I can't have children.

MAN: I wouldn't put it like that. You're probably as fertile as the next woman.

SALLY: Then why not?

MAN: I'm not saying that you mustn't. Ultimately it's your decision.

SALLY: But you think it's better I don't?

MAN: Pregnancy produces a hormone reaction in the woman's body. We can't tell how it may affect any cancer cells you might have lying dormant. Maybe there would be no reaction, maybe there would be a reaction. We don't know yet. So you have to decide.

SALLY: So I could?

MAN: Yes.

SALLY: And I have to decide?

MAN: Yes. And I'll give you any facts you need to make that decision.

SALLY: When do you think they'll find an answer? Something definite.

MAN: We don't know. But we're finding things all the time and we've already given you more of that.

Fifty

SALLY: Always there are the dark moments, the bad ones when I wonder why they bothered. And why I didn't just waste away and what fate has allowed me to continue. I want to go out like a light, but to shine very brightly before the dark. It is the little moments when I think, if they hadn't done a mastectomy I might not be here, having these moments, that they might not have happened at all because I hadn't been there. Then I think what does it matter that a breast is not there, because I am alive.

Tissue

I just sort of fell into being commissioned to write *Tissue*. I was on the 'phone to Birmingham Arts Lab about some royalties from *Want-Ad*, a play I had done there the previous year and they asked me if I was interested in writing a play for them as they were looking for a woman writer for a season of plays they were planning. As a new writer I was hardly in a position to say no. The Arts Lab suggested I went and talked to Kate Crutchley and Nancy Diuguid who were involved in doing the season of plays. We met at the Institute of Contemporary Arts in London. Nancy was going to direct whatever play I wrote. We talked about ideas. They wanted something specifically feminist. Nancy and Kate's feminism was far more radical than mine. We talked about body images. I've always been interested in advertising. I started off talking about facial disfigurement and somehow that idea turned more and more inward. The idea of something hidden. I think we must have got onto personal things about our own body images. I remember saying something about the way I felt assaulted by naked stomachs when I was on the tube because I have bad abdominal scarring. We got on to breasts because they were such a universal symbol of womanhood. I was a bit worried about working with Nancy because we have different sexual politics and I was hardly aware that I had sexual politics at all. But having thought and talked about the idea of writing a play about breast cancer I was very keen to write *Tissue*.

I didn't have long to write the first draft. Just over eight weeks which is much less time than I like to have. I wrote the first draft entirely from academic research. I always write researched plays by reading, doing a draft and then going and talking to people. I am a sucker for a good story and if I go to individuals first I get too involved with them to be objective. I wrote the first draft and Nancy read it. I don't think she cared for it much. She didn't think I'd got close enough to some aspects of women's experience. She suggested I took a tape recorder and recorded interviews with women who had had breast cancer. I got in touch with the mastectomy association who put me in touch with several of their members. These are women who are prepared to talk about their mastectomies in order to help other women. Women who are prepared to talk about the experience of having cancer and having their breasts removed are women who to some extent have come to terms with that experience. This slanted the research as I was not talking to women who were not so well adjusted. But once I started talking openly about writing a play on mastectomy, women whom I had no idea had had mastectomies, began to confide their experiences to me. I began to understand more and more the taboo nature of the subject I was writing about and how much women wanted the subject discussed.

The play wasn't easy to write. I was very conscious that the theme was a heavy one. That is why the children's scenes are in the play. Scene Twelve, when Sally and Zoey are trying to make their breasts grow makes the audience laugh; it also reminds them of the way girls build up body images of themselves. There have been criticisms that the play is too morbid, particularly the scene where Sally's boss talks about his wife's losing fight with cancer. But a play on a subject like breast cancer has to be honest. Not everybody wins.

About two weeks before rehearsals started I came up with a script which I discussed with the actors. We read the script through and began to talk about it. The company had been together for some weeks before I joined them and I think it was difficult for them and for myself when I first arrived with the script. They didn't know how much they could say or not about it and I didn't know how they would feel about the script. Good ideas came out of the first meeting and I went off to rewrite the play.

We started rehearsing in London. The first couple of days we did a lot of talking. There were a lot of things which we had to free in ourselves. It was hard to start talking deeply about the questions the play raised. We had to trust each other first. It was a relief to get through the first week and move to Birmingham for the rest of the rehearsals. The break we had between London and Birmingham did us good. We were pleased to see each other. And we'd all got caught up in the play. The production had begun to matter as much to the actors, Kate Crutchley, Michael Cassidy and Elizabeth Revil, as it did to Nancy and myself. It still wasn't an easy time. Not for any of us. There were some bad days when we all argued. Not with each other but because we were desperate to get the play right. I was very tired. I was rehearsing all day and then rewriting in the evenings often until 2 or 3 am. Sometimes things which had seemed good ideas when we'd tried them the day before didn't work when I had written them down and we'd go through the whole scene again and again trying to capture a moment or feeling. There's never enough time for rehearsing any play. Sometimes we felt we were running against the clock. The actors all put in more time than their contracts asked for. One day, when we were at a very low ebb, rehearsing in the foyer of the Arts Lab instead of the large, light gym we had been using, a member of the Birmingham branch mastectomy association came in to talk to us. The actors wanted to meet a woman who had had the experience of breast cancer and who would answer their questions. The discussion started off rather slowly and was fairly routine until Michael asked what an artificial breast was like. The woman who was talking to us immediately took hers out of her bra and handed it to him. Silence. It was a very real moment for us all. We passed the artificial breast between us and the thing we all noticed was its warmth and weight. We talked a long time after that. Our contact saw a rehearsal of the play and though she had criticisms of the play, was very positive about it. It did us all a lot of good to hear a judgement which came from outside ourselves. And from someone who had inside knowledge of the subject.

The production was very simple. Early on Nancy and I talked of only using a few props. Nancy wanted to use very specific things like the grapes which Zoey brings. During the rehearsals we discovered that we didn't need props. The actors had an ability to use the words for the motivations they required. Not using props gave the production a liquidity which I loved. The production captured the fluidity which remembered thought has. The set, designed by James Helps, came out of discussions with all of us. We had only limited space so needed a small set. There were money problems so we needed a cheap set. The answer to these problems was a sloping rectangular, almost square floor which was set up on the floor of wherever we were performing. The floor was painted white and had an open circle marked out on it by blue rope. At the openings to the circle the ropes led upwards, making thin supports for the actors and a token doorway. The only thing on the set was a polystyrene block, covered in canvas and lytex to strengthen it. This block could represent a bed, chair, table and anything else which was necessary. Because it was light there were no problems about moving it. The actors could pick it up and place it wherever they needed it for a scene. The costumes also had to be simple. We wanted to dress Michael and Kate who were playing Man and Woman as much the same as possible. No easy task as Mike is tall and Kate small. They were sent out to find something they both liked and came in both their sizes. They wore off-white shirts and blue cord jeans. Elizabeth, consistent in the role of Sally, had a dress. It was sort of mauve pink. A smock type dress which she could wear as a nightie, little girl's dress and a going out dress. I didn't want Sally ever to be seen naked. It was important that the audience knew she carried the trauma of mastectomy but that it was unseen. It was a company in which we all did everything. I made the dress.

The play opened in the Studio Theatre of Coventry Belgrade. I was amazed at its power to affect people. None of us expected the play to make people cry. It was only the third play I had written and I was surprised that it came over so strongly. I remember my mother saying during the performance, 'I wouldn't know it was by you.' At first after the performance we had discussions about the subject matter of the play. A lot of women felt inhibited by these and would say nothing during them but pour their hearts out in the bar. Perhaps we should have had women only discussions, but at the time I thought it important that men could also take part. We had a collection of the various prostheses so that women who had had mastectomies could know what was available. Everyone was always anxious to see these. They were passed round the audience so that they could feel the weight of them. I think that really brought home to people the physical sense of losing a breast. Later we dropped the discussions but made a point of being around after the play so we could talk to people who wanted to discuss the subject. The play went to the Studio of the Birmingham Repertory Theatre and in July 1978 to the ICA Theatre in London. The most gratifying thing about the production was not the clapping at the end of the performances but the people who came up to us and thanked us. It was a humbling experience.

The credit for getting *Tissue* produced on the radio belongs to radio drama producer, Vanessa Whitburn. It hadn't really entered my head that the play might be suitable for radio. Partly because of its style and partly because of the subject matter. *Tissue* was originally talked about in terms of a Radio 3 production but I was keen for it to go out on Radio 4 in the afternoon. I felt that the afternoon audience was the most captive audience and the listeners most unlikely to be informed about health care for women. Plays on Radio 4 tend to reach larger audiences than those on Radio 3 and like any writer I wanted my play to reach as many people as possible. I was amazed how easily the play transferred to radio. Alterations had of course to be made. It would have been impossibly confusing for the listeners had all the parts other than Sally been played by the same actors. The script had to be rewritten identifying individual characters instead of just Man or Woman. This then allowed Vanessa to cast actors with different vocal qualities as different characters, thus orchestrating the play.

The play had also to be cut to make it the required length for the Radio 4 afternoon theatre slot. In the end not as many cuts as I had pencilled in had to be made. Plays run faster on the radio than on stage. Scenes Fourteen and Forty-five went altogether and some other scenes were cut. It was not such a problem cutting scenes for the radio production as it had been for the theatre production. Because one can use different radio techniques such as cross fades and sound effects it is easier to make transitions between short scenes on the radio than it is in theatre. In the theatre production the changes into new scenes had to be very carefully written in to prevent the play from looking jumpy. The lyrical quality which came over in the radio production pleased me a lot. It's a quality that can't be captured in theatre in the same way. Using just vocal techniques to put the play across to the audience made it interesting to be involved with the play again so soon after its original production. I liked the aural quality produced by sometimes using sound effects and sometimes not. Using different microphones, the technicalities of radio allowed Sally (Jennie Linden) to have an inner and outer voice. This was a particularly effective way to convey her thoughts. *Tissue* was broadcast on 23 November 1978.

If I wrote a play now about mastectomy it would come out very differently to *Tissue*. Medical research into cancer has moved on and the links between breast and other forms of cancer and psychology is beginning to be quite extensively explored. I would certainly now go more deeply into this theory of cancer. My interest in the subject has not waned since I wrote the play. I still read all the articles I can find on the subject with as much interest as when I first started researching *Tissue*. My feminism has established itself more as I have got older; I was twenty-three when I wrote the play. I would automatically write a woman doctor now, it wouldn't have to be suggested to me by Nancy that it might be a good idea to make one of the doctors a woman.

After *Tissue* and *Lucy* (which is about euthanasia) I could have gone on writing about the health service and traumatic medical matters for a long time. Those were the sort of plays people knew I could write and which they kept asking me to go on writing. It took me a long time to have the courage to break away from those sort of subjects entirely. I began to realise that I didn't want to be typecast as a writer. I want to write about all sorts of subjects. About things which affect both men and women. This is why I choose not to work with groups that perform to women-only audiences. I think it is important that men are shown, in the way in which only theatre can show, the problems that women face in their lives.

I have always wanted to be a writer, since I could first write at the age of five. I decided I wanted to be a playwright when I was thirteen after being profoundly affected by John McGrath's *Events While Guarding the Bofors Gun*. Up until then I'd gone to the theatre really because I liked the costumes. But I came out of that Saturday matinee thinking, 'So that's what plays can do to people'. By the time I got home I had decided to be a playwright. There were no female writers that I was conscious of. I didn't see a stage play written by a woman until *Dusa, Fish, Stas and Vi*. I had read *A Taste of Honey* and it didn't strike me as strange that it was written by a woman but neither did it strike me as strange that there were so many plays written by men. It never occurred to me that as a woman I couldn't be a playwright. It took me a long time to realise that that was a contrary philosophy to the one with which a lot of women were brought up. I've only had about two days in my life when I've had any doubt that I could write plays. On those two days I could have thrown myself off the nearest bridge. I write plays because I want to say things. Writing is the most magical thing I know.

Louise Page

Louise Page

Stage Plays

Want-Ad (Birmingham Arts Lab 1977). Nick, an ambitious young journalist, exploits and distorts Sheila's tragic story to promote his own ends.

Tissue (Coventry 1978). A fast-moving impressionistic play about the trauma of mastectomy and the reactions to it.

Lucy (Playwrights Company, Bristol 1979). Explores the emotional and psychological problems when a young girl is hospitalised and gradually approaches death.

Hearing (Birmingham Rep 1979). Looks at the isolation caused by deafness and noise-induced hearing loss.

Flaws (Sheffield University Drama Studio 1980). A family bakery threatened with bankruptcy realises it has a far more serious problem on its hands.

House Wives (Derby Playhouse 1981). A woman's move from conservatism to standing for election for the Labour Party.

AURORA LEIGH

Dramatised from the verse-novel by Elizabeth Barrett Browning.

Aurora Leigh was first produced by Mrs Worthington's Daughters at the Young Vic Theatre in September 1979, with the following cast:

AURORA LEIGH	Marilyn Finlay
AUNT/LADY WALDEMAR	Anne Engel
ROMNEY LEIGH	Stephen Ley
MARIAN ERLE	Stacey Charlesworth

Directed by Julie Holledge
Designed by Mary Moore
Music by Jenny Sprince
Lighting by John Daniels
Technician Miriam Dorman

The version of the play printed here was produced as a rehearsed reading in the Olivier auditorium of the National Theatre on 14 April 1981, with the following cast:

AURORA LEIGH	Felicity Kendal
AUNT	Mary Macleod
ROMNEY LEIGH	Greg Hicks
LADY WALDEMAR	Anna Carteret
MARIAN ERLE	Caroline Embling

Directed by Nicholas Wright

AURORA: Of writing many books there is no end
And I who have written much in prose and verse
For others' uses, will write now for mine –
Will write my story for my better self,
As when you paint your portrait for a friend.

My story leaps across a century –
An epic tale, such as critics say has
Died out with Agamemnon and the Greeks.
I'll not believe it. All men are possible
Heroes – ay, and women too, heroines.

My mother was a Florentine
Whose rare blue eyes were shut from seeing me
When scarcely I was four years old. Father
Was an austere Englishman, with a great
Thirst for learning. Father and I, Aurora
Leigh, lived happy in Italy many years.
Then Father too died. There ended childhood.

Now I was alone; England beckoned.

AUNT: Aurora; welcome home, child.

AURORA: My father's sister; brown hair pricked with grey,
A nose drawn sharply, yet in delicate lines;
A close, mild mouth, a little soured about
The ends, from living a virtuous life,
A sort of cage-bird life, born in a cage
Accounting that to leap from perch to perch
Is act and joy enough for any bird.

AUNT: I loved your father and would love you too
As long as you deserve it.

AURORA: That is kind.

AUNT: As your father's child, you will speak his tongue.
Learn the collects and the catechism
Because I like instructed piety.
Learn your complement of classic French
And German also, since I like a range
Of liberal education – tongues, not books.

AURORA: I learnt a little mathematics; I
Washed in landscapes (or say rather, washed out).
I danced the polka and modelled flowers in wax
Because she liked accomplishments in girls.
I read a score of books on womanhood
To prove, if women do not think themselves,
They may teach thinking; books demonstrating
Their right of comprehending husband's talk
When not too deep, and even of answering
With pretty 'May it please you', or 'So it is',
As long as they keep quiet by the fire
And never say 'No' when the world says 'Yes'.

AUNT: I like a woman to be womanly
                  And English women, thank God, are models
                  To the universe. Aurora.

AURORA: Here, Aunt.

AUNT: Romney Leigh, your cousin. Your elder by
                  A few years and one day to be master
                  Of Leigh Hall. Tall and rather shy. You'll see.

ROMNEY: Good day, cousin. I see you take pleasure
                  In our English nature. 'Tis not too tame?

AURORA: Italy was one thing, England another;
                  Not a grand nature. Not my chestnut woods
                  Of Vallombrosa, cleaving by the spurs
                  To the precipices.

ROMNEY: I see you look for the gods, Aurora.

AURORA: Sometimes I get up early, just to sit
                  And watch the morning quicken in the grey
                  And hear the silence open like a flower
                  Leaf after leaf. Then read my books; for when
                  We gloriously forget ourselves and plunge
                  Soul forward, headlong into a book's profound,
                  Impassioned for its beauty and salt of truth –
                  'Tis then we get right good from a book.

ROMNEY: You look indeed for the gods, Aurora.

AURORA: The world of books is still the world, Romney.

ROMNEY: You speak so of the poets and don't laugh?
                  Those virtuous liars, dreamers after
                  Dark, soothsayers in a tea-cup.

AURORA: I speak
                  Of the only truth-tellers. While common
                  Men build houses, gauge railroads, reap and dine
                  And dust the flaunty carpets of the world,
                  The poet suddenly will catch them up
                  With a voice like a thunder.

ROMNEY: Oh, delight
                  And triumph of the poet.

AURORA: That name is
                  Royal, and I tingle like a queen to
                  Think I might sign my name to't. All I can
                  Say is that I write to live, live to write.

I passed much time with Romney, also with
His close painter friend, Vincent Carrington,
The three of us as lively thinkers met;
We read or talked or quarrelled as it chanced.
More often, Romney Leigh and I, alone.

AUNT: Aurora, have you done your crochet yet?

AURORA: And so through forced work and spontaneous work
                The inner life informs the outer life.

                            ****

AURORA: I stand upon the brink of twenty years –
                Woman and artist; either incomplete.

ROMNEY: The earliest of Auroras: I greet you.

AURORA: Let's keep my birthday till my aunt awakes.
                What, therefore, if I crown myself today?

ROMNEY: What branches will you choose?

AURORA: I choose not bay –
                Nor myrtle – which means chiefly love; and love
                Is something awful which one dares not touch
                So early o'mornings. Ah, there's my choice:
                That headlong ivy. Not a leaf will grow
                But thinking of a wreath.

ROMNEY: Here's a book I found. No name writ in it.
                I saw at once the thing had witchcraft in't,
                Whereof the reading calls up dangerous spirits.
                I rather bring it to the witch.

AURORA: Romney,
                Thank you.

ROMNEY: My thanks rather go to you,
                Fair cousin, that I have seen you not too much
                Witch, scholar, poet, dreamer and the rest –
                To be a woman also.

AURORA: Poets must be
                Either men or women, more's the pity.

ROMNEY: But men – and still less, women – happily
                Scarce need be poets. Keep to the green wreath,
                Since e'en dreaming of the stone and bronze
                Brings headaches, pretty cousin.

AURORA: I perceive
The headache is too noble for my sex.
You think the heartache would sound decenter?
Since that's the woman's special, proper ache
And altogether tolerable – except
To a woman.

ROMNEY: Aurora, pray throw by
This game of argument. Life is too grave.

You write as well . . . and ill . . . upon the whole
As other women. If as well, what then?
If even a little better . . . still, what then?
Your woman's heart can't hold this world of woe.
Your sympathies towards the human race
To you means such a child, or such a man
You saw one morning waiting in the cold.

You may write of factories and of slaves as if
Your father were a negro and your son
A spinner in the mills. But does one woman
Of you stand still from dancing, pine and die
Because of this general suffering?
This universal anguish? This same world,
Uncomprehended by you, must remain
Uninfluenced by you. Women as you are,
Mere women, personal and passionate –
You give us doting mothers and chaste wives,
Sublime Madonnas and enduring saints;
We get no Christ from you – and verily,
We shall not get a poet, to my mind.

For you, Aurora, with the large, broad brow
And steady eyelids, cannot condescend
To play at art as children play at swords.
You never can be satisfied with praise
Which men give women when they judge a book
Not as mere work, but as mere women's work,
Expressing the comparative respect
Which means the absolute scorn:
'Among our female writers we make room
For this fair writer, and congratulate
The country that produces in these times
Such women, so competent to . . . spell.'

AURORA: Do you see the world so bad, my cousin?

ROMNEY: May I vow away my years and my means
Among the helpers, for the common blood
That swings along my veins is strong enough
To draw me to this duty.

AURORA: You believe
In God?

ROMNEY: I sympathise with man, not God,
And when I stand beside a dying bed,

It's death to me. I am as men are, not
As men may be hereafter.

AURORA: I'm young in age, and younger still, I think,
As a woman. A woman's younger than
A man, at equal years, because she's barred
Maturing by the outdoor sun and air
And kept in long clothes past the age to walk.

Ah well. I know you men judge otherwise:
You think a woman ripens as a peach,
In the cheeks, chiefly. I can't loose the knot
Of social questions. But I can applaud
August compassion, Christian thoughts that shoot
Beyond the vulgar pale of personal aims.
Accept my reverence.

ROMNEY: No other help?

AURORA: You would scorn my help because a woman's?

ROMNEY: I ask for help that only you can give.
I ask for love – and that a woman can
For life in fellowship – wifehood. Will she?

AURORA: Now may God be witness; am I proved weak
To stand alone, yet strong enough to bear
Such leaners on my shoulders? Poor to think,
Yet rich enough to sympathise with thought?
Incompetent to sing, as blackbirds can,
Yet competent to love, like you?
It's always so. Anything does for a wife.

ROMNEY: Aurora dear – and most dearly honoured,
You translate me ill. If your sex is weak
For art, it is all the more fit and strong
For life and duty. Place your fecund heart
In mine, and hand in hand we'll go where you
Will touch life's victims one by one, until
The shape of every man will have a name
And every woman catch your mother's face
To melt you into passion.

AURORA: What you love
Is not a woman, Romney, but a cause.
Your cause is noble, your ends excellent,
But I, being most unworthy of these and that,
Do otherwise conceive of love. Farewell.

ROMNEY: You reject me thus?

AURORA: You forget too much
That every creature, female as the male,
Stands single in responsible act and thought.

For I too have work to do; though your world
Were twice as wretched as you represent.
Most serious work, most necessary work
As any economist's reform. What then
Unless the artist keep up open roads
Betwixt the seen and unseen, unless the
Artist reaches for what's beyond speech, through
Imagination? I'll not barter the
Beautiful for barley. Perhaps my soul
Aspires, does not create. Yet I aspire.

AUNT: Aurora. Romney. Come, my child, entreat
Your cousin to the house and have your talk –
If girls must talk upon their birthdays. Come.

ROMNEY: The talk is ended, madam, where we stand.
Your brother's daughter has dismissed me here;
And all my answer can be better said
Beneath the trees, than wrong by such a word
Your house's hospitalities. Farewell.

AUNT: You have dismissed my guest?

AURORA: I little thought
To give dismissal to a guest of yours,
In letting go a friend of mine who came
To take me into service as a wife.

AUNT: You cannot mean to tell me to my face
That Romney Leigh has asked you for his wife
And you refused him?

AURORA: Did he indeed ask?
I think he rather stooped to take me up
For certain uses which he found to do
For something he called a wife. He never asked.

AUNT: What is it that you want, before you'll step
One footstep for the noblest lover born?

AURORA: I am born to walk another way, Aunt.

AUNT: You walk, you walk. A babe at thirteen months
Will walk as well as you. You think you are
So rich and free to choose a way to walk?

It was your father set you where you are,
An undowered orphan. Your father wrote
Directly on your birth to wed you to
Romney. I cannot inherit, being
A woman – and nor can you. The Hall and
Grounds are Romney's when I die. You cannot
Eat or drink or stand or sit or even
Die like any decent wretch without your

Cousin Romney. Hall, grounds – are his when I die.
(Except a few books and a pair of shawls.)

You love this man. I've watched you when he came
And when he went and when we've talked of him.

But stay now. I write a word and counter
This sin.

AURORA: My father's sister, hear my word
Before you write yours. You may mean me well,
But my soul is not a pauper; I live
At least my soul's life, without alms from men.

AUNT: We'll leave Italian manners, if you please.
I think you had an English father, child,
And ought to find it possible to speak
A quiet 'Yes' or 'No', like English girls.

AURORA: I care for Romney, Aunt. But love for him
Is an arrangement; a legal contract
Drawn by his father. If I married him
I would not dare to call my soul my own
Which he had so bought for; every thought
And every heartbeat down there on the bill.

****

AURORA: The next week passed in silence, and the next
And several after. Romney did not come
Nor my aunt chide me. I lived on and on
As if my heart were kept beneath glass
And everybody stood all eyes and ears
To see and hear it tick. Neighbours dropped in
And talked with measured, emphasised reserve
Of Parish news, like doctors to the sick . . .

But on the sixth week – my aunt, oh, my aunt.

****

ROMNEY: The will gives you all the personal goods
And three hundred pounds from your aunt.

AURORA: I thank
Her memory for that. With three hundred pounds
I buy in England, even, clear standing room
To stand and work in.

ROMNEY: And see, the will says
'Such other sums of which she died possessed.'
She died possessed of thirty thousand pounds.

AURORA: My aunt possessed this sum? Inherited
From whom and when?

ROMNEY: I said she died possessed
              Of this, dear cousin.

AURORA: Not by heritage.
              Thank you. We're getting to the facts at last.

ROMNEY: The facts are not afraid of hurting you.
              You'll find no cause in all your scruples, why
              Your aunt should cavil at a deed of gift
              'Twixt her and me.

AURORA: Ah, I thought so. A gift.

ROMNEY: A very natural gift.

AURORA: Meant plainly for
              Her heirs. I am snared then. But cousin, shall
              I pardon you if thus you have caught me?

ROMNEY: Is't my fault, mine, that you're a wild creature
              Of the woods and hate the stall built for you?
              I do not hold the cords of your wide net.
              You're free from me, Aurora.

AURORA: Your gift was
              Tendered . . . when? Accepted when?

ROMNEY: The day before her death-day, you will find
              The gift was in her hands.

AURORA: We've reached the top
              Of this steep question and may rest, I think
              For mark, a letter, unread, mark – still sealed,
              Was found enfolded in the poor dead hand.
              Here's a proof of gift, but here's no proof, sir
              Of acceptancy.

ROMNEY: May I ask your plans?

AURORA: I'm open to you, cousin. I go hence
              To London, to the gathering place of souls,
              To live mine straight out, vocally, in books.
              Harmoniously for others, if indeed
              A woman's soul, like man's, be wide enough
              To carry the whole octave. That's to prove.
              Pray God be with me, Romney.

                         ****

AURORA: When Romney Leigh and I had parted thus
              I took a chamber up three flights of stairs
              And, in a certain house in Kensington,
              Three years I lived and worked. Get leave to work

In this world – for women to work, 'tis best.

****

AURORA:

Serene and unafraid of solitude,
I work the short days out. I do some
Excellent things indifferently, some
Bad things excellently. Both are praised –
The latter loudest. I watch the large sun
On lurid mornings or monstrous afternoons
Push out through the cloud with his dilated disc
And startle the slant roofs and chimney pots
With splashes of fierce colour. Or I see
Fog only, the great tawny, weltering fog,
Involve the passive city, strangle it
Alive and draw it off into the void:
Spires, bridges, streets and squares, as if a sponge
Has wiped out London.

        Being poor, I am
Constrained for life to work with one hand for
The booksellers, working with the other
For myself and art. I apprehend this:
In England no one lives by verse, that lives.
And, apprehending, I resolve by prose
To make a space to sphere my living verse.
I write for cyclopedias, magazines
And weekly papers. I learn the deft use
Of the editorial 'We' in a review –

LADY WALDEMAR:

Lady Waldemar. Is this, then, the Muse?

AURORA:

There's none here. I – I fail to guess the cause
Which taxed you with this visit, Madam?

LADY WALDEMAR:

Good. For I like to be sincere at once.

Perhaps if I had found a literal Muse
The visit might have taxed me. As it is,
You wear your blue so chiefly in your eyes,
My fair Aurora, in a frank good way,
It comforts me entirely for your fame
As well as for the trouble of my ascent
To this Olympus.

AURORA:

        But your ladyship,
You leave me curious – ?

LADY WALDEMAR:

          Is blue in eyes
As awful as in stockings, after all?
I think you have a cousin, Romney Leigh.

AURORA:

You bring word from him?

LADY WALDEMAR:

         More word about him.
You do not love him?

AURORA: You are frank at least
In putting questions, Madam. I can say
I love my cousin – cousinly. No more.

LADY WALDEMAR: I guessed as much. I'm ready to be frank.
'Tis I love Romney Leigh.

AURORA: Forebear, I beg –

LADY WALDEMAR: I love your cousin. If it seems unwise
To say so, it's still foolisher (we're frank)
To feel so. My first husband left me young
And pretty enough, so please you, and rich enough
To keep my house in Mayfair with the rest.
And I'll tell you straight, there are marquises
Would serve seven years to call me wife, I know;
And after seven I might consider it,
For there's some comfort in a marquisate.

But I love Romney. You put up your lip –
So like a Leigh, so like him. Pardon me,
I am well aware – the name is good,
The means are excellent. But the man, the man –
Heaven help us both. I am near as mad as he
In loving such an one.

AURORA: I see you now.
For me, I do believe in love and God.
I know my cousin; Lady Waldemar
I know not.

LADY WALDEMAR: You speak grave, like a prophetess
Who knits her brows across her pretty eyes
To keep them back from following the grey flight
Of doves between the temple-columns. Dear,
Be kinder with me. Let us two be friends.
I'm a mere woman, the more weak, perhaps,
Through being so proud. You're better; as for him,
He's best –

AURORA: I own myself
Incredulous of confidence like this
Availing him or you.

LADY WALDEMAR: And I myself
Of being worthy of him with any love,
And yet I save him if I marry him.
But let that pass.

AURORA: Pass – pass? We play police
Upon my cousin's life to indicate
What may or may not pass?

LADY WALDEMAR: Now let's talk reason, though we talk of love.

Your cousin Romney Leigh's a monster. There.
The word's out fairly. Let me prove the fact.
With godlike virtues and heroic aims
Of mismade human nature. Grant the man
Twice godlike, twice heroic – still he limps,
And here's the point we come to.

AURORA: Pardon me,
But Lady Waldemar, the point's the thing
We never come to.

LADY WALDEMAR: Caustic, insolent –
I like you. And now, my lioness,
For all your roaring, help me. For myself,
I would not say so – but for him, for him.
A week hence – so I lose him – so he is lost.
And when he's fairly married, he a Leigh,
To a girl of doubtful life, undoubtful birth,
Starved out in London, till her coarse-grained hands
Are whiter than her morals – you for one
May call his choice most worthy.

AURORA: Married – lost?

LADY WALDEMAR: You're moved at last; I can see from your face.
Sure you must know your Leigh by heart. If you're
Not starving, you're nothing to him. But come
Fit for the parish stocks and Romney's there
To call you brother, sister, or perhaps
A tenderer name still. For me, I've done
What women may – I've done my best, read half
Fourier, Proudhon, Marx – socialists!
And if I had been a fathom less in love
Had cured myself with reading. As it was
I quoted from them prettily enough,
Learnt by heart his speeches in the Commons
Upon the social question; heaped
Reports of wicked women and penitentiaries –
'Twas well to see a woman of my class
With such a dawn of conscience – but for him –
He cannot tell the colour of my hair.

AURORA: Then is there really a marriage?

LADY WALDEMAR: Miss Leigh,
I spoke to him of this he holds secret.

'He would not choose,' I said, 'that even his kin,
Aurora Leigh, even, should conceive his act.'
He grew so pale, dear, to the lips, I knew
I had touched him. 'Do you know her?' he inquired,
'My cousin Aurora?' 'Yes,' I said, and lied
(But truly we all know you by your books),
And so I offered to come straight to you,
Explain the subject, justify the cause

And take you with me to St Margaret's Court
To see this miracle, this Marian Erle,
This drover's daughter (she's not pretty, he swears)
Upon whose fingers, exquisitely pricked
By a hundred needles, we're to hang the tie
'Twixt class and class in England. He thanked me
And promised as my reward to put off
His marriage for a month.

AURORA:

I understand your drift imperfectly.
You wish to lead me to my cousin's betrothed?
So be it then. But how this serves your ends
And how the strange confession of your love
Serves this, I have yet to learn.

LADY WALDEMAR:

                              Then despite,
Aurora, that most radiant morning name,
You're as dull as any London afternoon.

I wanted time – and gained it; wanted you –
And gain you. I beg – break this marriage up.
We'll plant a better fortune in its place.

Be good to me, Aurora, scorn me less
For saying the thing I should not. I have kept
The iron rule of womanly reserve
In lip and life till now. I wept a week
Before I came here.

AURORA:

                              Your love's curable,
Lady Waldemar.

LADY WALDEMAR:

                              You are hard, Miss Leigh.
Forgive me that I rashly blew the dust
Up before your eyes. You find probably
No evil in this marriage, rather good.
You'll give this love your signature, perhaps?

AURORA:

Who tells you that he wants a wife to love?
There's work for wives as well. For me, you err
Supposing power in me to break this match.
I could not do it to save Romney's life,
And would not, to save mine.

LADY WALDEMAR:

                              Farewell, then. Write
Your books in peace. I mistook the way here.

****

AURORA:

Two hours afterward I was within
St Margaret's Court, to meet this Marian.

****

MARIAN: My father earned his life by random jobs
               Despised by steadier workmen – keeping swine
               On commons, picking hops or hurrying on
               The harvest at wet seasons. In between
               He cursed his wife because without money
               She could not buy more drink; at which she turned
               And beat her child – me – in revenge for her
               Own broken heart. Mister Leigh, your cousin,
               Considered truly that such things should change.

               But let those early years pass from me now.

               After I came to London, I fell ill.
               I lay and seethed in a fever many weeks,
               A heap of misery in a hospital.
               One day, the last before I left the place,
               A visitor was ushered through the wards –

ROMNEY: And you, my dear, where will you go from here?
               And how came you in this place before me?

MARIAN: And so we met anew and met again
               Until at last he said:

ROMNEY: We shall not part,
               Dear Marian. My fellow worker – be my
               Wife.

AURORA: So indeed he loves you, Marian?

MARIAN: Why, he loves all. He had not asked me else
               To work with him for ever and be his wife.

AURORA: With women of my class, 'tis otherwise.
               We haggle with the small change of our gold,
               And so much love accord, for so much love.
               If marriage be a contract, look to it, then:
               Contracting parties should be equal: just.

MARIAN: Are you vexed at me
               Because your cousin takes me for a wife?
               I know I am not worthy – nay, in truth,
               I'm glad on't, since for that he chooses me,
               He likes the poor things of the world the best.
               I'll be a worthier mate perhaps than some
               Who are wooed in silk among their learned books
               For they're hard sometimes, despite their white hands.

ROMNEY: Aurora, you're here.

AURORA: Lady Waldemar
               Has sent me in haste to find a cousin of mine
               Who shall be.

ROMNEY: Lady Waldemar is good.

AURORA: Here's one at least who is good. I've sat here
                 And learnt the thing by heart, and from my heart
                 Am therefore competent to give you thanks
                 For such a cousin.

ROMNEY: You accept at last
                 A gift from me, Aurora, without scorn?

AURORA: You cannot please a woman against her will;
                 And once you vexed me. Shall we speak of that?
                 I comprehend your choice – I justify
                 Your right in choosing.

ROMNEY: No, no, you cannot
                 Comprehend my choice, my ends, nor myself.
                 But I thank you for your praise this time.

AURORA: Well, cousin Romney, be happy. Perhaps
                 Marian may be married from my house?

ROMNEY: I take my wife directly from the people;
                 We'll wear no mask as if we blushed for shame.

AURORA: Dear cousin Romney – you're the poet.

                             ****

AURORA: A month passed so, and then the notice came:
                 On such a day, the marriage at the church.

                 I've waked and slept through many nights and days
                 Since then – but still that day will catch my breath
                 Like a nightmare. The lame, the blind and worse
                 Pressed in upon the church. Noble ladies
                 With 'broidered hems of perfumed handkerchiefs
                 Pressed to their noses stood in the tall pews.

                 We waited. It was early. There was time.

                             ****

ROMNEY: My friends, bear with me. There's no marriage.
                 She leaves me. My pardon – you are all dismissed.

MARIAN: Dear Romney: be patient with me. I know
                 I'm foolish, but there might be some truth here.
                 Very kind to me was Lady Waldemar.
                 She came to see me nine times, rather ten;
                 So beautiful she hurt me like the day
                 Let suddenly on sick eyes. Most kind of all
                 Your cousin. She kissed me; I felt her soul

Dip through her serious lips in holy fire.

God help me, but it made me arrogant.
I almost told her that you would not lose
By taking me to wife.

I never could be happy as your wife;
I never could be harmless as your friend.
I cannot thank you for the good you did.
My dear Romney – my hand shakes – I am blind –
I'm poor at writing at best. Your Marian.

AURORA: Romney, my dear.

ROMNEY: I thank you, Aurora.
          Your printers' devils have not spoilt your heart.

****

AURORA: I laboured on alone, the wind, dust
          And sun of the world blist'ring in my face.

****

AURORA: How dreary 'tis for women to sit still
          The winter nights by solitary fires
          And think for comfort how, that very night,
          Affianced lovers, leaning face to face
          Are reading haply from some page of ours,
          To pause with a thrill, as if their cheeks had touched –
          To have our books appraised and linked to love
          While we sit loveless.

Here's a poet – and he has a mother.
Another, and he a wife. Who loves me?

Yet so I will not. This vile woman's way
Of trailing garments shall not trip me up.
I'll have no traffic with the personal thought
In art's pure terrain. Must I work in vain
Without the approbation of a man?
It cannot be; it shall not.

Tonight I go abroad for once. Into
The lights and talkers of Lord Howe's grand house.

LADY WALDEMAR: Miss Leigh – I have word to speak to you
          About your cousin's place in Shropshire –

AURORA: I have not seen Romney Leigh these two years.
          They say he's very busy with good works,
          Has parted Leigh Hall into almshouses.

LADY WALDEMAR: I've been to see his work – our work – you heard
          I went? You'll like to hear your books lie there,
          As judged innocuous for the elder girls.

So said Romney, who might have been poet
Until he saw much higher things to do.

AURORA: How she talks to pain me: a woman's spite.
A woman takes a housewife from her breast
And plucks the delicatest needle out
As 'twere a rose, and pricks you carefully
'Neath nails, 'neath eyelids, in your nostrils –
A beast would roar, so tortured; but I, I,
A human creature, must not, shall not flinch.

LADY WALDEMAR: I think he looks quite well now – he's quite got
Over that unfortunate, wretched girl . . .

AURORA: 'Tis clear my cousin Romney needs a wife.
So, good. She tells me clearer than in words.

Dear Lady Waldemar, I could not speak
For joy of the great news that I hear
Of you and my cousin. May you be
Most happy, and the good he means the world
Replenish his own life. You need not write.
My book is done, and that labour now o'er,
I think of leaving London, England even,
And hastening to get nearer to the sun
Where men sleep better. So, adieu.

****

AURORA: Such glittering boulevards, such white colonnades
Of fair fantastic Paris; her fountains
In the sunshine, as bright dice, sure to win.

Here I wait, till my good friend Carrington
Bargains for my book with the publisher
And sends all the proceeds here, to me.

I walk the days out, listening to the chink
Of the first Napoleon's dry bones,
Musing how love of beauty makes us shrink
And draws us backward from the coarse town sights
To count the daisies upon dappled fields.

Marian? Is that Marian's face? On this street –
Why, what would Marian do in this great town?

Marian – it is you.

MARIAN: Let pass.

AURORA: I lost a
Sister many days –

MARIAN: You speak as kind as
One I knew before.

AURORA: Are you ill? Or tired?

MARIAN: There's one at home has need of me. Let pass.

AURORA: Marian, it is I – Aurora Leigh.

MARIAN: You'll not find the Marian whom you left before,
            But a woman with a child, a son.

AURORA: Child –

MARIAN: He is all mine. I have as sure a right
            As any glad proud mother in the world
            Who sets her darling down to cut his teeth
            Upon her church-ring. I claim my mother-dues
            By common law, by which the poor and weak
            Are trodden underfoot by vicious men.

AURORA: I thought a child was given to sanctify
            A woman – to set her in the sight of all.

MARIAN: What have you in your soul against me? Why,
            All of you? Am I wicked, do you think?
            God knows me, trusts me with the child – but you,
            You think me really wicked.

AURORA: Complacent
            To a wrong you've done when you left the place
            Of a noble heart to take the hand of
            A seducer.

MARIAN: Of whom? I was never
            As you say – seduced.

AURORA: Oh, pardon my thoughts –

MARIAN: I'm glad you clear me so. My heart's a stone
            Except where it is touched as a mother.
            Just a mother; only for the child am
            I warm and cold, and hungry and afraid
            And smell the flowers a little and see the sun.
            Do not treat me as if I were alive,
            For though you ran a pin into my soul
            I think it would not hurt or trouble me.

AURORA: When he had lost you, sought you, missed you still,
            He drew the curtains of the world awhile.

MARIAN: But soon his love for Lady Waldemar –

AURORA: Love? What do you know of his love for her?

MARIAN: Promise me now that he will never learn
            In what a dreadful trap this creature here
            Has him caught. From that long day she first came
            I saw things different, felt new mistrust.
            'Twas plain a man like Romney Leigh, she said,
            Required a wife more level to himself.
            Leaning to me she told me tenderly
            That she knew of knowledge, without a doubt,
            That Romney Leigh had loved her formerly,
            And though I stood between her heart and heaven,
            She loved me wholly. But my fate was clear:
            Instant passage abroad and full money.
            The rest is short. I wrote the letter which
            Delivered him from me. When I came here
            My clothes, money, all were stolen. My life
            Was like before, this time among strange tongues
            And ways of violence. A man's violence,
            Not man's seduction made me what I am.

AURORA: Why, how one does weep when one's too weary.

            So hard for women to keep pace with men –
            As well give up at once, sit down at once,
            And weep as you do. Tears, tears. Why we weep?
            That we've shamed a life, lost a love, missed a
            World? Simply that we've walked too far
            Or talked too much, or felt the wind i' th'east.

            Come, Marian. I am lonely now, and you
            Are lonely, and the child –

            Dear Lady Waldemar; I'm very glad
            I never liked you, which you knew so well.
            I know now how you tricked poor Marian Erle.
            If haply you're the wife of Romney Leigh,
            I charge you, be his faithful and true wife;
            Thus you are safe from Marian and myself,
            We'll stir no dangerous embers. Fail a point –
            And so I warn you. Yours, Aurora Leigh.

                        ****

AURORA: The next day we took train for Italy.

            I found a house at Florence, on a hill;
            The Vallombrosan mountains to the right,
            Which sunrise fills as full as crystal cups,
            Wine-filled and red to the brim. No sun
            Could die unseen by dwellers at my villa.
            After some time passed, word came from Vincent.

                        ****

MARIAN: 'We think here, that you have written a good book
            And you a woman. It was in you, that
            Which still from female finger-tips burns blue.'

AURORA: 'A good book,' says he, 'and you a woman.'
The book has some truth in it, I believe,
And I a woman. Feebly, partially,
Inaptly in presentation, Romney'll add,
Because a woman –

MARIAN: 'When the fever took your cousin at first,
Just after I had writ to you in France,
They tell me Lady Waldemar mixed drinks
And counted grains, like any salaried nurse –
Excepting that she wept too.' Between these
Lines it seems they must be married and he
Likes not to tell you straight.

AURORA: And I – I have come back to an empty nest
Which every bird's too wise for. Do I hear
My father's step on this deserted ground,
His voice along the silence, as he tells
The name of bird and insect, tree and flower
And all the presentations of the stars.

MARIAN: Your father's house, Aurora, is not yours.
See, not a stone of wall uncovered now.
Vine leaves, other dwellers –

****

AURORA: Many an eve
I wander the valley, like a brief ghost.
This perfect solitude of foreign lands,
A new world, all alive with people new
And am possessed by none of them. No right
In one to call your name, inquire your where,
Or what you think of Mr Someone's book
Or Mr Other's marriage or decease,
Or how's the headache which you had last week?

At such times ended seems my trade of verse.
I do not write or read or even think,
But sit absorbed amid the quickening glooms
Dropped in by chance to a bowl of water
To spoil the drink a little and lose itself,
Dissolving slowly, slowly, until lost.

ROMNEY: Aurora –

AURORA: Romney.

ROMNEY: I have travelled far.

AURORA: Is Lady Waldemar with you?

ROMNEY: I have
Her letter.

AURORA: That you are come is wonder.

ROMNEY: And Marian? She's well?

AURORA: You know she's here, then?

ROMNEY: I heard account of her in the village.

AURORA: She's well.

ROMNEY: I – have read your book, Aurora.

AURORA: You have read it and I have writ it. So?

ROMNEY: My daily bread tastes of your book. It lives,
               Dreams and wakes in me. Better than best wine.

AURORA: The book lived in me 'ere it lived in you.
               I know it closer than another does
               And it's unworthy so much compliment.
               Beseech you, keep your wine, and when you drink
               Still wish some happier fortune to your friend
               Than even to have written a far better book.

ROMNEY: This book stands above me and draws me up.
               I will not say there are not, young or old,
               Male writers – ay, or female – let it pass –
               Who'll write us richer and completer books.
               Enough that this one book has looked at me.

AURORA: I mind me of a far-off June, when once
               On my birthday we discoursed of life and art.
               Now, if I had known, that morning in the dew
               My cousin Romney would have said such words
               On such a night at close of many years
               In speaking of a future book of mine,
               It would have pleased me better as a hope.

ROMNEY: I've come here, to speak my soul out to you.
               Once I was truculent in assumption,
               Quite absolute in dogma, proud in aim
               And fierce in expectation. I, who felt
               The whole world tugging at my hands for help
               As if no other man than I could help,
               Nor woman, but I led her by the hand.
               I know myself tonight for what I was.
               That birthday, poet, 'twas you talked so right
               While I – I built up follies like a wall
               To intercept the sunshine and your face.

AURORA: Speak wisely now.

ROMNEY: Then I beheld the world
                As one great famishing carnivorous mouth,
                A huge deserted callow blackbird Thing,
                With piteous open beak that hurt my heart.
                The words you spoke to me then –

AURORA: 'What then
                Unless the artist keep up open roads
                Betwixt the seen and unseen –'

ROMNEY: I failed then
                In setting right society's wide wrong
                Because not poet enough to understand
                That life develops from within.

AURORA;   I have
                Failed too.

ROMNEY: But you are a great writer now.

AURORA: You've read my book but not my heart. I know
                I've failed, if failure means to walk away
                And look back sadly on work gladly done.
                That June day you too spoke words as truthful
                As mine. And if I had shown a gentler
                Spirit, less arrogance, it had not hurt me.

ROMNEY: Oh best Aurora, are you then so sad
                You scarcely had been sadder as my wife?

AURORA: Your wife, sir? I must certainly be changed
                If I, Aurora, can have said such things.

ROMNEY: You misunderstand me –

AURORA: I'm glad of it.
                Ten years of birthdays on a woman's head
                Are apt to fossilise her girlish mirth.

                Perhaps I doubt more now than you doubted then.
                I think, when the sun shines, that I've failed.
                But what then? Though we fail indeed, we have
                Our work to do. We should be ashamed to
                Sit here, so impatient that we're nothing.

ROMNEY: I now think God will have his work done
                And that we need not be disturbed too much
                For Romney Leigh or others having failed,
                Wanting perfect heroism without a scratch.

AURORA: No honest work of man or woman 'fails';
                It feeds the sum of all human action.

Did all your social labour at Leigh Hall
And elsewhere, come to nought then?

ROMNEY: The men and women of disordered lives,
Whom I brought in order to dine and sleep,
All broke the waxen masks I made them wear
And cursed me for my tyrannous constraint
In forcing crooked creatures to live straight.

The county's hounds were set upon my back
To bite and tear me for my wicked deed
Of trying to do good without the Church.
I had my windows broken once or twice,
By Liberal peasants, naturally incensed
At such a vexer of Arcadian peace
Who would not let men call their wives their own
To kick like Britons. Why, I brought from town
The wicked London tavern-thieves and drabs
To affront the blessed hillside drabs and thieves
With mended morals. My windows paid for't.
I was shot at once and pelted often
In riding through the village. 'There he goes,
Who'd drive away our Christian gentlefolk
In that pernicious prison, Leigh Hall,
With all his murderers. Give another name
And say Leigh Hell, and burn it up with fire.'

AURORA: What, burn Leigh Hall?

ROMNEY: You never heard, cousin?
They did it quite perfectly. Let us grant
'Tis somewhat easier to burn a house
Than build a system. When the roof fell in
The fire paused, stunned for but a moment
Beneath the stroke of slates and the tumbling
And then rose up at once and roared
And wrapped the whole house inside a mounting
Whirlwind of dilated flame. In my dreams
I still hear the silence after. So still,
So silent that you heard a young bird fall
From the top nest in the neighbouring rookery

AURORA: Leigh Hall . . . gone.

ROMNEY: 'Twould have made a fine sight for
A poet, to make the verse blaze after.

AURORA: I shall not from the window of my room
Catch sight of those old chimneys any more.
A foolish fancy. Does it make you smile?

ROMNEY: No fancy. 'Tis a great charred circle where
The patient earth was singed an acre round,
With one stone stair, symbolic of my life,
Ascending, winding, leading up to nought.

AURORA: I think you were ill too?

ROMNEY: So ill, I wished
To end completely. But I failed to die
As formerly I failed to live. I thought
To ponder on another grave question:
Is it right to wed here, while you love there?
I will not vex you any more tonight,
But having spoken what I came to say,
The rest shall please you. What she can, in me,
Protection, tender liking, freedom, ease,
She shall have –

AURORA: In the old days a farewell
Was soon said. Since then I've writ a book or two;
I'm plain at speech, direct in purpose; when
I speak, you'll take the meaning as it is,
And not allow for puckerings in the silks
By clever stitches. Now mark me well, sir –
They burnt Leigh Hall. Well, that is as it is.
Tonight you've mocked me somewhat – or yourself –
And I at least have not deserved it so.
I wish you well through all the acts of life
And life's relations, wedlock not the least.
And it shall 'please me', in your words, to know
You yield your wife protection, freedom, ease
And very tender liking. May you live
So happy with her, Romney, that your friends
May praise her for it.

The lady never was a friend of mine,
Good cousin, therefore both for her and you
I'll never spoil your dark nor dull your noon.
Indeed, 'twould shake a house if such as I
Came in, to acknowledge palm to warm palm
The mistress there – the Lady Waldemar.

ROMNEY: What name's that you spoke?

AURORA: Why, your wife, Romney.

ROMNEY: Are we mad? Wife? Mine? Lady Waldemar?
May God judge me so. I came here today
Sorely humbled. Because this one woman
Had shown me something which a man calls light,
Because too, formerly I sinned by her
Through arrogance of my masculine ways.
And thus I came here to abase myself
And fasten, kneeling, on her regent brows,
A garland which I startled thence one day
Of her beautiful June youth.

Are you the Aurora who made large my dreams
To frame your greatness? You conceive so small?
At last, then, peerless cousin, we're peers.
Men have burned my house, maligned my motives
But not one has wronged my soul as you have,

	Who called the Lady Waldemar my wife.

AURORA: Not married to her? But you said –

ROMNEY:
                                    Nay, here,
Read these lines she sent you through me.

LADY WALDEMAR: I prayed your cousin Leigh to take you this.
When watching at his bedside fourteen days,
He broke out ever like a flame at whiles
Between the fever.

ROMNEY:
                        Aurora – bring her book,
And read it softly, Lady Waldemar,
Until I thank your friendship.

LADY WALDEMAR:
                            So I read
Your book, Aurora, for an hour, that day;
I kept its pauses, marked its emphasis.
My voice, empaled upon rhyme's golden hooks,
Not once would writhe, nor quiver, nor revolt.
I read on calmly, calmly, shut it up.

There is indeed some merit in the book,
And yet the merit in't is thrown away
As chances still with women, if we write
Or write not. Good morning, Mr Leigh,
You'll find another reader next time.
Male poets are preferable, tiring less
And teaching more. I ask for your pardon,
For having done no better than to love
And that not wisely. I took some trouble
For your sake, because I knew you did not
Love Marian. I meant the best – for you
And me and her. I am sorry for't.

ROMNEY: 'Tis true? Henceforth Marian must be my wife.

LADY WALDEMAR: He's just, your cousin; ay, abhorrently.
He'd wash his hands in blood, to keep them clean.

I'll have no more business with blood in my veins,
Not even to keep the colour at my lip.
A rose is pink and pretty without blood –
Why not a woman? When we've played in vain
The game to adore, we have resources still,
And can play on at leisure, being adored.

Henceforth I'll admit no socialist
Within three crinolines, to love and have
His being. But for you, he might be mine,
And to you I have shown my naked heart,
For which two things, I hate, hate and hate you.

AURORA: Not married?

ROMNEY: You mistake. Is not Marian
          My wife? I have a wife and child, 'fore God.

MARIAN: You take this Marian, such as wicked men
          Have made her, for your honourable wife?

ROMNEY: I take her as God made her, and as men
          Must fail to unmake her, for my honoured wife.

MARIAN: You take this Marian's child, which is her shame,
          Of whom you will not ever feel ashamed?

ROMNEY: May God so father me as I will him –
          To share my cup, to slumber on my knee,
          To hold my hand in all the public ways.

MARIAN: And you, Aurora? Will you blame me much
          If, careful for that outcast child of mine
          I catch this hand that's stretched to me and him?

          You've been my friend, and you're his cousin too;
          And I'll be bound by only you in this.

AURORA: Here's my hand to clasp yours, Marian, as pure
          As I'm a woman and a Leigh. Witness
          That Romney Leigh is honoured in his choice
          Who chooses Marian for his honoured wife.

MARIAN: My thanks, Aurora. And you, my generous
          Friend, although you seem unchanged, and having
          Promised faith to me, maintain it as if
          I were not changed, yet I cannot wed you.

          The truth is, I am grown so proud with grief,
          I've come to learn – a woman, poor or rich,
          Despised or honoured, is a human soul,
          Although she should be spit upon by men.
          And so you see me. Oh, it does me good
          That Romney Leigh should think me worthy still.

          I do not love you.

          Perhaps, my friend, I set you up so high,
          Above all actual good or hope of good,
          I haply set you above love itself?
          But if indeed I loved, 'twas well before
          I heard my child cry in the desert night
          And knew he had no father. It may be
          I'm not as strong as other women are;
          It may be I'm colder than the dead.

          I could not bear to see my child upon
          Your knee, and know by such a look or sigh
          Or such a silence that you thought smetimes:
          'This child was fathered by some cursed wretch.'
          Can you think I'd have another baby,
          A fathered child, to vex my darling when

He's asked his name and has no answer for't?

I've room for no more children in my arms.
My hand shall keep clean, with no marriage ring,
To tend my son till he cease to need me.

ROMNEY: You see now, Aurora, I had come here
Bound Marian's, bound to keep the bond and give
My name, my house, my hand, the things I could
To Marian. Now I see – she needs me not
And here is ended my pretension. But
I have a truth to tell, and scarce know how
To tell it –

AURORA: My words are all gone from me.

ROMNEY: I have said much. Farewell, Aurora dear.

AURORA: But when a woman says she loves a man –
The man must hear her –

ROMNEY: Aurora.

AURORA: Oh, I
Would not be a plain woman like the rest.
I must analyse, confront and question.

In this last I have not changed and could not.
But in one respect I see I am changed.
Marian saw, and Lady Waldemar saw
What I was too proud and dishonest to
See: that I loved you then and love you now.
I should have died so, crushing in my hand
This rose of love, the wasp inside and all.

ROMNEY: When I was still a boy, I was oft told
Of how a faery bride from Italy
With smells of oleanders in her hair
Was coming through the vines to touch my hand.

AURORA: That, Romney, is but romance.

ROMNEY: Yet we're here.
Later I dreamed I would bring down my bride,
The dust of golden lilies on her feet,
That she should walk beside me on the rocks,
And help the work of help which was my world.

AURORA: The world of books is still the world, Romney.

ROMNEY: And you still live to write, and write to live?

AURORA: I write to live – yes; but live to live too.

And see that we are, as men and women
Are, and not as we may be hereafter.

ROMNEY: Do we now walk the same way, Aurora?

AURORA: If we still leave room for a working noon.

ROMNEY: And you, Marian, you'll stay? Your child
May have his father, with no fear for him
Or you.

AURORA: Two mothers and a father now;
He's rich as no child has been before him.

****

AURORA: My tale ends here for you. I have discerned
My age and spoken of my time to yours.
My art and work sets action on top of
Suffering; the world of books is still the world,
The artist's part is both to be and do.
The Greeks said grandly in their tragic phrase:
'Let no-one be called happy till their death',
To which I add: 'Let no-one till their death
Be called unhappy.' Measure not the work
Until the day's out and the labour done.
Deal with us nobly, women as we be,
And honour us with truth, perhaps with praise.

****

Aurora Leigh

Until the early 1970s I knew little about Elizabeth Barrett Browning. I had read some of her love sonnets and vaguely thought of her as a languishing Victorian lady, dominated by a tyrannical father, and carried to freedom by romantic poet Robert. I wasn't terribly interested in his poetry. Then, in about 1972 I read an article by American feminist critic Elaine Showalter. She was discussing the work of past women writers, and she quoted from *Aurora Leigh*. When I came across a second-hand copy of Mrs Browning's (sic) complete works, I remembered her reference. I was at the time on the look-out for second-hand books by women writers to whom I had been led by other feminist literary research.

I ploughed through *Aurora* – and I say ploughed because it was very hard going. Not just because of its length (2,000 lines longer than Milton's *Paradise Lost*, I later learned) but because of the tiny print and the sheer difficulty of nineteenth-century iambic pentameter. It was rhetorical, discursive, florid and hard often to disentangle the story from the elaborations. Like most other people, I'm not in the habit of perusing epic poems for my bedtime reading – my pleasure in demanding writers like Shakespeare, Donne and Hopkins had been carefully helped at school, university and in the case of the first, in performance.

I returned to the poem in 1976, and found my reactions much stronger. This time I could follow the story and I was very excited by the verse-novel's ambition, by its subject matter, and this time, by the verse itself. It is far broader in its concerns than I could make room for in my dramatisation – it debates the social function of art – realist or escapist; it discourses on Christianity, socialism, Victorian philanthropy, republicanism, as well as feminism, economic independence for women, motherhood and (indirectly) sexuality. The core story – that of a woman trying to make her independent way in life – was lively and moving. I decided I wanted to do something more with it than read it for pleasure, and decided to try and dramatise it. It was very hard work, but tremendously exciting.

I wanted to make the story active and dramatic, retaining Aurora as the dramatic centre of the play. So, as in the original verse-novel, she remained the narrator. I also wanted to keep the iambic line, and to work with it myself. Although I write poetry, I had not yet dared to write a play in verse. Because I had had mixed responses myself, I wanted to make it accessible, so that people could either enjoy the play for its own sake, or go off and read the original if their appetite was whetted. It was a long and painstaking process, even though I was working with already given material. I read and re-read it, becoming familiar with patterns of imagery – particularly the clusters of 'feminine' imagery, using nature, embroidery, in a subversive way, so that Aurora is turning the passive nature imagery with which women have been objectified in men's love poetry into an active weapon as part of her struggle for autonomy.

I had a problem with the end. In the original Romney is blinded (à la Rochester) in the fire that destroys his home and his philanthropic work. I tussled with this for a long time, because I felt I couldn't render the meaning of the end neutrally. Romney loses everything, and comes to find Aurora to declare himself totally wrong and her totally right. His blindness is profoundly symbolic – his darkness against Aurora's light. But as a feminist I found it impossible to accept such capitulation as representing any real resolution.

If Aurora and Romney's reconciliation were to have real potential for equality in the future, I could not see how it could be credible if male domination was simply replaced with female domination. I could see why Elizabeth Barrett might have had to overstate her case – through taking both poetic and polemical licence, but it seemed to me that a contemporary audience would either want Aurora to reject Romney completely, or, in today's more liberal times, would need to believe that Romney still had something going for him. And after all, he does come to her, and it is her achievement, which are the subject of the play. I felt that by keeping Romney's sight, I was retaining the spirit of the original ending, while departing from its letter.

In the spring of 1977 I sent the play to BBC radio, the National Theatre and the Royal Shakespeare Company. I did that deliberately, since I wanted the play done by people who had a tradition of dealing with dramatic verse. I think I hoped that the interest in classical form (ie. verse drama) might alert people to my rediscovery of a work by an undervalued English writer. The BBC returned the play with a puzzled 'But it isn't a play, really, is it?' My National Theatre contact offered: 'But it isn't exactly Pushkin, is it?' to which the only honest reply was 'No, it isn't exactly Pushkin'. The RSC returned it after two years with no comment at all, which led me to suspect it hadn't been read by anyone. I was fed up.

Then, in early 1979, I mentioned the play to a fringe group called Mrs Worthington's Daughters. They had formed in 1978 to present plays 'by or about women' from the past. They took it on, and toured the play in autumn 1979. The BBC radio producer saw their production and said it was now much better, since I had rewritten it. I answered that I hadn't rewritten at all, merely cut about four pages from its 110 minutes. The play was bought for radio, cut to 80 minutes, and broadcast on Radio 3 in 1981.

Encouraged by this, I resubmitted it to the National Theatre in autumn 1980. This time it was read with sensitivity by Nicholas Wright, who directed it as a rehearsed reading in the Olivier in April 1981, after further cuts and a little reshaping. That is the version published here.

I'm telling the story of the play's journey into production because I think it throws light on some of the difficulties playwrights have, and women playwrights in particular. Any writer will sympathise with the frustration of sending out a play you know will work and not getting a sympathetic reading of it. But I had two other problems; the first was that my last plays had been performed in London in 1975. I had gone back to university to do an MA, and although I knew I was still a playwright, I felt I had to start from scratch as a writer, putting myself on the theatrical map for other people who had forgotten I wrote plays. Secondly, I think that in 1977 the theatre was still very riddled with gender-blindness. Very few women writers were having their work performed, 'feminism' was a dirty word in most theatre criticism, and theatres were not, as they are beginning to now, acknowledging the relative absence of plays either about women or from women's point of view. Though these 'classical' theatre institutions were primed to deal with the form of *Aurora*, they were not primed to respond to its content. It took a fringe company in which the women were feminists to approach the play via its content – and hence to be prepared to take on what very few fringe groups have done; a verse play.

Later, of course, with the play validated in performance, with more feminist groups and more women writers around, *Aurora* had more of a context. It is a real-life irony that my experience to some extent paralleled the experience of Aurora herself; although women today have professional and personal freedoms of which Elizabeth Barrett Browning might not have dreamt, the old prejudices and ignorances are still there and will still take a long time to break down.

I had different responses to the different productions. Mary Moore designed a white, abstract set for Mrs Worthington's Daughters, which swept up at one corner, and had chairs placed at the other corners. Jenny Sprince wrote some haunting string-music motifs to counterpoint the action, and her music was also used for the radio production. It was a daring production, subject to the hassles of touring and working for very little money. Inevitably the performances had ups and downs, as I think is bound to happen with a play which is so demanding in itself, and where the touring group have all the other functional and administrative things to worry about as well. But the production had the simplicity and fluency which I love in the theatre. Time and space were completely flexible; I still find the most exciting theatre is very often that in which naturalistic paraphernalia are at an absolute minimum, so that the audience's attention is on what happens between the people in the shared imaginative world onstage.

The Platform Performances at the National Theatre were very different; staged simply, with two rows of chairs, the cast in modern dress, it worked superbly well. The elegance and passion of the language were simultaneously simple and sophisticated. It was one of the most rewarding experiences of my last ten years as a playwright. The pivot of the play anyway is Aurora herself; she controls it – narrating, re-enacting, commenting. She is a woman in charge of her life and of a work of art – both in the fact that it is her story, and her structural function in the play. She must have poise, passion and wit.

The text has no scene divisions or stage directions. The language is clear about *what* happens; it is up to the director to decide *how* it happens. Because of its structure the play demands a fluent pace, but apart from that it is up for grabs. It is a very rich text, and verbal and physical gestures have to be discovered through an understanding of the language. If that understanding doesn't happen, then no amount of stage directions from me can compensate. So I haven't even put in exits and entrances, since characters do not necessarily have to go off.

Elizabeth Barrett Browning called *Aurora Leigh* 'the most mature of my works, and the one into which my highest convictions upon Life and Art have entered'. Although the original poem was first published as long ago as 1857, and although it is clearly a feminist work, the story of a woman in charge of her life (and the epic form), it is also a play which via its social and gender specificity also explores the relationship between aspiration and achievement. It is about personal struggle and cultural voice; and that makes it immediate and relevant, as well as historical and literary. And I am very fond of it.

Michelene Wandor

Michelene Wandor

Stage Plays

The Day After Yesterday (Act Inn Theatre Club 1972). About sexual/moral hypocrisy, centring on 'Miss World' contest.

Spilt Milk (Portable Theatre Workshop 1973). Surreal play about pressures on mothers. Published in *Play Nine* (Edward Arnold 1981).

To Die Among Friends (Paradise Foundry 1974). Five dialogues on inter- and intra-sexual politics. Published in *Sink Songs* (Playbooks 1976).

Penthesilea (Salt Theatre 1977). Adaptation of Kleist play about the Amazons.

The Old Wives' Tale (Soho Poly 1977). About three women on the verge of retirement.

Care and Control (Gay Sweatshop 1977). About women and custody. Published in *Strike While the Iron is Hot* (Journeyman Press 1981).

Floorshow (Monstrous Regiment 1977). Sketches and lyrics on women and work.

Whores D'Oeuvres (Omoro 1978). Surreal play about two prostitutes adrift on a raft in the Thames. (Published in 'Hecate', 1980).

Scissors (Almost Free 1978). Jewish family comedy.

AID Thy Neighbour (Theatre at New End 1978). Comedy on contemporary attitudes to parenthood.

Correspondence (ICA 1979). A divorced woman reassesses her life.

Aurora Leigh (Mrs Worthington's Daughters 1979). Adaptation of Elizabeth Barrett Browning's verse novel about a woman writer.

The Blind Goddess (Red Ladder 1981). Adaptation of Toller play on justice and morality.

UNDERSTUDIES
Theatre and sexual politics

Michelene Wandor

'The whole aspect of sexuality in the theatre has, at last, been given an airing by Michelene Wandor in a direct and provocative investigation into sexual politics in the British theatre, particularly during the 1970s. She examines feminism and homosexuality, placing their treatment in a social, historical and political context. She writes, furthermore, as much for those who are unfamiliar with or hostile to sexual politics, as for those who are already aware of the struggle to express sexuality on stage . . . Michelene Wandor has made a radical analysis without appearing aesthetically raw or politically simple' Catherine Paice, *Plays and Players*.

'This excellent book . . . recognizes that theatre is a barometer of the social climate and shows how the battles that have raged around sexuality throughout this century have been reflected on its stage . . . It's a must. Buy it' Noel Greig, *Gay News*.

'By design a slim volume – only 88 pages long – but it certainly packs a punch. Not only is it an analysis of sexual politics in modern theatre, but it also serves as a history of feminist and gay theatre over the last 13 years' Sarah Dunant, *Spare Rib*.